THIS MEANS MORE

THIS MEANS MORE

IT'S BIGGER THAN ME

NINA EVANS

This Means More Book Reviews

"Nina Evans captures the essence of truth in transition in a piercing account of her journey to emotional, financial, and spiritual freedom. This book had me begging for more!"

—**Pastor Dallas Blacklock**

"*This Means More* is a brilliantly written work that gives an account of a young woman growing in faith as she gains a deeper understanding and appreciation of the love of Christ through intentional reflection on the events of her life. She reveals that what may seem like coincidences or just events to some are actual evidence of God's unconditional and unfailing love, protection, and guidance. The author challenges the reader with questions that invoke spiritual discernment and the revelation of the constant little miracles that piece together the life of a believer."

—**Denecia Davis**

"We have all suffered loss, love, and health but you have collectively put together a teaching tool to let us know that God is still in the blessing business. We have to understand that we (YOU) are a blessing to others and embrace those moments and build on them."

—**Dr. Dwalah Fisher**

"*This Means More* is an inspired read that will cause you to evaluate your purpose. To see the move of God and how obedience can change the trajectory of several lives is amazing. You will be abundantly blessed and challenged to see things from a new perspective."

—**Gabrielle Floyd**

"Nina, I want to thank you personally for trusting God when He tasked you with writing *This Means More* because it will bless so many people who need a push in their faith toward all God has in store for them!! Obedience over sacrifice!!!"

—**Syreeta Blacklock**

This Means More: It's Bigger Than Me

Copyright© 2021 Nina Evans

All rights reserved. No part of this book may be reproduced or transmitted in any form, without the written permission of the publisher, except for brief quotations for review purposes.

Scripture quotations taken from the Amplified® Bible (AMP), Copyright © 2015 by The Lockman Foundation. Used wby permission. www.lockman.org

Scriptures marked NKJV are taken from the NEW KING JAMES VERSION (NKJV): Scripture taken from the NEW KING JAMES VERSION®. Copyright© 1982 by Thomas Nelson, Inc. Used by permission. All rights reserved.

Scripture quotations marked (NIV) are taken from the Holy Bible, New International Version®, NIV®. Copyright© 1973, 1978, 1984, 2011 by Biblica, Inc.™ Used by permission of Zondervan. All rights reserved worldwide. www.zondervan.com The "NIV" and "New International Version" are trademarks registered in the United States Patent and Trademark Office by Biblica, Inc.™

Published by
ELOHAI International Publishing & Media
P.O. Box 1883
Cypress, Texas 77410
elohaipublishing.com

ISBN: 978-1-953535-30-6

Printed in the United States of America

Dedication

This book is dedicated to the little girl inside of me (and all of us) who has so much to say but has been afraid to speak up for most of her life. It is time to speak up and use your voice.

Table of Contents

Acknowledgments xi
Introduction 1
Chapter 1: Growing Up 3
Chapter 2: The Parentals 7
Chapter 3: My Brother's Legacy 13
Chapter 4: Sister, Sister 17
Chapter 5: Financial Freedom 23
Chapter 6: Community 29
Chapter 7: We All Need Therapy 33
Chapter 8: Destined to Be an Accountant 37
Chapter 9: A Little Here, There, and Everywhere 43
Chapter 10: Relationships 49
Chapter 11: The Athlete 55
Chapter 12 : My HBCU Experience 61
Chapter 13: Travel, Travel, Travel 65
Chapter 14: Crazy Faith 71
Chapter 15: Life Abroad 77
Chapter 16: The Year 2020 85
Chapter 17: The Restoration Process 91
Chapter 18: A Life of Faith 95
Let's Connect 97
Financial Coaching 98
About the Author 99

Acknowledgments

With God, nothing is impossible. Because of his goodness, grace, and mercy, I am here today. My life starts and ends with him; he is my firm foundation. I am forever grateful for his unwavering love for me. Even when I do not think I am worthy, he reminds me that I am. I will always praise him and lift up his holy name because of who he is. All the praise, glory, and honor is due to him.

To the Hillcrest Church family, thank you for investing in me as a child and introducing me to Jesus. This has made an incredible difference in my life. Your investment will now go out and impact nations.

To my community, who has encouraged me, prayed for me, and called to check on me, thank you! I could not have done this without you. You all believed in me when I did not believe in myself. I was not sure I could do this, but you all continued to push me, and I am thankful for each one of you.

Introduction

Have you ever taken inventory of your life and its many different puzzle pieces? The puzzle pieces represent various aspects—every friend, family member, and foe; every decision you have made (good or bad); how you grew up; everything you completed or started but did not finish; every job you have worked; every situation you endured; and every person you have encountered. It also includes your personality traits, where you are gifted, your interests, your strengths and weaknesses, and what you are passionate about. All of our puzzle pieces are coming together to form the bigger picture that we celebrate as our life. The puzzle pieces are not random and did not happen by mere coincidence. I believe God has orchestrated and ordained each piece to fit perfectly together. He is sovereign and in control of it all. *Yours, O LORD, is the greatness, the power and the glory, the victory and the majesty; For all that is in heaven and in earth is Yours; Yours is the kingdom, O LORD, and You are exalted as head over all. Both riches and honor come from You, And You reign over all. In Your hand is power and might; In Your hand it is to make great and to give strength to all* (1 Chronicles 29:11-12).

When you begin to think about the puzzle pieces of your life, how does it make you feel? As I reflect on my own life, I now understand that this means more—it is bigger than me and, in fact, has very little to do with me. The trials, tribulations, and triumphs I have experienced mean more. They are all part of God's divine plan and purpose. The puzzle pieces are coming together to complete the bigger picture. I am reminded and live by Romans 8:28 (AMP), which says, *And we know [with great confidence] that God [who is deeply concerned about us] causes all things to work together [as a plan] for good for those who love God, to those who are called according to his plan and purpose.* I invite you to take this journey with me as I reflect on the puzzle pieces of my life. Some pieces will make you smile, and some will make you uncomfortable, but I pray through it all you see God's goodness, grace, love, and mercy and will take the time to reflect on your own personal journey to see God's hand on and through your life and gain a fresh perspective for your puzzle. Revelation 12:11 (NKJV) says, *And they overcame him by the blood of the Lamb and by the word of their testimony, and they did not love their lives to the death.*

CHAPTER 1

Growing Up

I was born and raised in a small country town in West Texas called Big Spring, Texas, located in Howard County. When I was growing up, the population was approximately 25,000. As of the quick facts report from the United States Census Bureau, the population estimates as of July 1, 2019 was approximately 28,000. The current demographics are approximately eighty percent White, ten percent Hispanic, seven percent Black, one percent Asian, one percent Indian, and one percent other, but those percentages were slightly different when I was growing up. This meant I did not have a lot of people around who looked like me.

The town had one kindergarten, two elementary schools, one middle school, one junior high, and one high school, and it is home to Howard College and the Southwest Collegiate Institute for the Deaf. Points of interests include Settle's Hotel, Comanche Trail Park, Delek US Refinery, and the former Webb Air Force base, just to name a few. Everyone knew each other and whose child you were. My family owned a small three-bedroom, one-bathroom house near Anderson Kindergarten School.

I have seven members in my family, including dad, mom, my brother, three sisters, and myself, who shared our home. My parents had their room, my brother had his own room (because he was the only boy), which meant all four girls shared a room in the approximate 900-square-foot house. We grew up always playing outside (but you better be inside before the streetlights came on). Since there were five children, we had no issues finding someone to play with, and we were surrounded by plenty of other kids our age in the neighborhood. When I was younger, our house was the gathering house. On the weekends, music was playing, the adults played dominoes and drank their "adult beverages" while laughing and talking, BBQ and plenty of food was flowing, and the children played fun games outside (Red Light Green Light, Hide-n-Seek, etc.). We had a good time and were a fun family.

My dad was a truck driver (on the road most of the week but home on weekends), and my mom was a store manager at Burger King. It was all fun and games while everyone was at the house, but behind closed doors, it was a different scenery. My parents fought a lot, with constant yelling and bickering. The yelling and fighting were so bad that I would go to my room and either hide in the closet or under the bed, plugging my ears and rocking until it stopped.

One Sunday morning, we were playing outside and the church van from Hillcrest Baptist Church was driving through our neighborhood. They stopped and asked if we wanted to attend church. Thankfully, our parents obliged us, and we hopped on the church van. This was my first experience and exposure to Christ. Children's church was so fun and engaging that we began to attend church, regularly relying on the church van to pick us up or, if we missed the van, then having my mom or dad drop us off. On a few occasions, I even walked to church because I did not want to miss it. We as children attended church, but my parents did not at this time.

We experienced the love of Christ like never before through the people of the church. No matter that their skin color was different than ours, these individuals embraced us, loved on us, and made us feel special. They often checked on us and always found a way to keep us involved. My parents could not financially afford to send all of us to church camp, but someone always sponsored us, so we could all attend each summer. This is when I began to fall in love with Christ. Although we had a lot of chaos at home, I found my peace at church, where I felt like I belonged. We stayed at Hillcrest until we graduated high school and moved away. This church family will always and forever hold a special place in my heart for introducing me to Christ and ensuring we stayed connected.

In middle school, I began to play sports. I played volleyball, basketball, and ran track. Volleyball and basketball were my favorites, and I quickly learned that track was not for me. Sports became another outlet, allowing me to focus on something other than the chaos at home. I had never played sports before, but thankfully, I was naturally athletic and learned the game quickly.

Playing sports at times reminded me of the madness at home when my parents would forget to pick me up after a game or practice and I was left sitting on the curbside waiting. Most of the time, I had to use the phone in the coach's office to call my mother to come get me, a teammate's parent asked if I needed a ride, or my coach took me home. A few times, I walked home, which was three or four miles. This often left me feeling abandoned and forgotten, but I refused to stop playing sports, and by high school, I learned how to determine my own transportation plans, not relying on others.

I knew sports was my ticket out of Big Spring, Texas. I despised being there, and in sixth grade, I determined in my heart that when I grew up, I'd never return. All the decisions and choices I have made in my life were fueled by the burning desire to never return to Big Spring. Even now in my older age, the thought of ever having to move back to West Texas makes me nauseous. I visit family usually once per year at Christmas or Thanksgiving, and I typically counted down the days to when I could return to Houston. To be clear, it is not the city itself but rather what it represented. It represented the chaos of my childhood, the place where I had my heart broken repeatedly by family, and the missing presence of my brother. Even visiting used to be very tough, but because I have gone through my healing process in therapy, I can now visit and enjoy hanging out with my family for a few days. My dad and one sister remain there today.

This means more... Being introduced to Christ at a young age has helped me to understand that God has always had a plan for my life. He is using what I experienced to become a launching pad for me to go out and impact the world. Where I lack, he fills. Where you lack, he will fill you also. Where you have experienced pain, he can heal and use you to help someone else. The people of Hillcrest were a shining light in my life, and just like them, we can be a shining light for someone else. You will find yourself giving in areas where you did not receive. For example, although I did not receive nurturing from my mother growing up, as a healed adult, I am a nurturer for my godchildren. I did not even know I could be a nurturer until God placed them in my life and I began caring for them and giving them what I did not receive. It came instinctively and, quite honestly, surprised me. The difference-maker was caring for them from a healed place instead of repeating the cycle of what I experienced.

What we experience in our childhood will show up in our adult lives. The decisions and choices we make are often fueled by those experiences. I have learned that although I do not have all fond memories of my childhood, I can heal those wounds, change how I see myself in the story, and make better decisions as an adult. This has inspired me to become an advocate for therapy and counseling because I wholeheartedly believe we all need therapy (regardless of whether our memories are good or bad). My memories are being used to propel me into my purpose of helping others. The lens on my perspective has been forever changed and I will continue to do my work to heal.

> ❖ **Reflect on your life:** As you think about your childhood, what kind of emotions come up? Would you consider seeking therapy to help process your thoughts and feelings? See how the experiences of your childhood have shaped your life and how you can use them for a greater purpose.

CHAPTER 2

The Parentals

My parents met at a young age and were together for almost twenty years before divorcing. My dad was born and raised in Midland, Texas, and my mom is from Lamesa, Texas. As far as I can remember, I have always been a daddy's girl who loved to learn from her father. He was always teaching me (yes, he showed me how to change my oil and my own tire, although I did not commit any of that to memory). While not everything has been easy and I definitely don't understand some things about him, I have always appreciated the lessons.

My dad was a provider as I was growing up. I now understand his love language is acts of service, which is no coincidence because that is mine also. He was not always physically present, but he was always pushing me to be better along the way. He ensured we had clothes on our backs and food to eat. He expected me to get straight A's and to give my all in everything I put my hands to. Regardless of the job—whether working at the convenience store as a clerk at sixteen years old or working as an accountant at age thirty-eight—his expectation of my work ethic has not changed. Give your all in all you do; never depend on anyone to take care of or provide for you, and go get all that is yours. I would not be who I am today without my daddy. I am thankful our relationship has evolved over the years, and we talk now both as friends and as father and daughter. Of course, I wish he had been more physically present and not so hard on me in my younger years which I have been able to discuss with him. He now says if he could turn back the hands of time, he would have been more physically present for his children. When I asked him why he is hard on me, he stated, "Because I know you can handle it, you are the strong one."

As we turn on the TV, watch the news, or read social media, we hear the world worshipping and always giving gratitude to the mothers. Most professional athletes and actors are always thanking their mothers for their contribution to their lives when acknowledging their successes. Mothers play a significant role in our lives because we would not be present in this world without them. They spend months and months carrying us in their wombs. As I think about that, it seems like the bond of a mother and her child would be indescribable. But a small percentage of us in the world do not have that type of loving and healthy bond with our mothers. Instead, that relationship can be filled with pain and disconnection.

For decades, I have struggled with the lack of a relationship with my mother. She was present in my adolescent years, often being at the center of chaos and confusion in our family. She and my dad fought frequently, leaving the house in disarray and us children trembling in fear. The fighting began to cease when my brother reminded my parents of the impact all the fighting and chaos was having on us children. I was extremely grateful for this, yet serious damage had already been done.

Fast forward to sometime later and my mother shifted from being physically present to being absent. This is certainly not meant to bash her, but I am sharing my experience and the pain I have carried for decades because of it. I recall the shift taking place when my mother became "a Christian" and joined her church. It seemed she stopped caring for her family in order to spend all her time at church. She became progressively combative with my dad verbally, and she wanted everyone else to change around her. All the things she and my dad did together and that we did as a family suddenly stopped because church had become the priority. I wondered how this could be. At a young age, I attended church and had my own relationship with God, so I knew that experience was not normal. The God I read about in the Bible and had come to know was different than what I was experiencing through my mother.

The Parentals

The disconnection and pain in our relationship continued to grow and grow. As the youngest of five children, my mother had given birth to me right before her nineteenth birthday. She was young and never really had an opportunity to live her life to the fullest, and I believe she gave us what she could. She was only repeating a generational cycle that has plagued our family. However, this still does not lessen the pain of feeling like you are not a priority to the woman who carried you and brought you into this world.

I remember being in the sixth grade and telling myself that I couldn't wait to grow up, leave all the chaos and dissension behind me, and never come back. Even at that age, I suppressed those emotions and continued to press on, striving to always do my best and give my all. I pressed on through high school. I was on the honor roll and was one of the top athletes. My dad attended none of my high school games and my mother attended maybe one or two. Even then, she criticized how I played instead of saying, "I'm proud of you for playing hard today." Oh, how I longed to just hear those words.

In my senior year of high school, I signed a national letter of intent to play volleyball at Cisco Junior College. My brother attended the signing day with me, and this was our last picture together because weeks later, he would drown in a lake while at college. The loss of my brother was devastating and hard for our entire family. We all grieved in our own way. Then a year later, my mom informed my dad that she was leaving him and wanted a divorce. This time of devastation and loss all at once was too much. To be honest, I just wanted to run away from life. The timing of going off to college was perfect because it meant I could be away from the turmoil.

I certainly tried running from all this pain most of my life but quickly learned that I had only become an expert at masking pain instead of dealing with it. During college, my relationship with my mother did not grow any closer. Our family went into our own silos and processed our pain separately. We did not really communicate about the impact of the loss of my brother and my parents' divorce. It has been two decades since my brother's passing, and it seems the relationship with my mother has only grown further apart.

For years, protecting my peace has been more important to me than allowing unhealthy people into my life. I have watched my mother gradually destroy most of the relationships in her life. She has attempted to create confusion among us siblings, which at times has succeeded, but we are working through our healing process as sisters together. I once tried to personally address these issues with her one-on-one but was met with defensiveness. It baffled me how someone could not self-reflect and take responsibility for what they have contributed to the lives of their children. I believe this is largely due to our family's generational cycle and curse between mother and daughter. My mother's actions are not new but only a repeat of what I believed happened with her mother.

On November 8, 2020, I had a dream I will never forget. During the days leading up to this, I had been praying heavily about breaking generational cycles and curses in my family. I had been speaking this prayer over my family:

> *Therefore, the Evans and Edwards family is no longer a slave but a son; if a son, then also an heir through God (Galatians 4:7). It is for freedom that Christ has set us free. Stand firm, then, and do not let yourselves be burdened again by a yoke of slavery (Galatians 5:1). My family is no longer bound by broken mother and daughter relationships or financial mismanagement (living paycheck to paycheck and mishandling our money); and no longer are we people who are deceitful, manipulators, and controllers.*

> *Therefore, if anyone is in Christ, the new creation has come; the old is gone; the new is here (2 Corinthians 5:17). The Spirit you received does not make you slaves so that you live in fear again, rather, the Spirit you received brought about your adoption to sonship, and by him we cry, Abba Father (Romans 8:15). Submit yourselves then to God. Resist the devil and he will flee from you (James 4:7).*

Therefore, I declare my family has been set free and we are no longer bound by those generational cycles and curses that have held us back. We are a people who are healthy and whole individuals in relationship with others; we are kind, gentle, honest, pure in heart, and trustworthy; and we have financial freedom and are building generational wealth.

After speaking this prayer repeatedly, I dreamed I was praying over my mother, and as I was speaking, demons came out of her. I looked them in the eyes, rebuked them, quoted scriptures mentioned in my prayer, and they fled. For the first time in my life, I was not scared by this experience but stood firm in my position. I exercised the authority and power given to me by Jesus Christ and called forth those negative things to leave. Immediately upon waking up that morning and vividly remembering that dream, I sent a voice memo to my mother, praying over her and our family. I specifically sent a voice memo because I wanted us to be able to play it repeatedly.

These generational curses, cycles, and habits have to stop, and for my family, it stops now. It is time to learn, grow, and heal. I decree and declare that healing is brought forth in my family. I decree that we are no longer bound by broken mother and daughter relationships, and we are becoming healthy individuals in relationship with one another. While I do not know if my relationship with my mother will ever improve, I do know that I can begin to break the cycle by seeking the counseling I need to process my childhood trauma and heal those wounds that go deeper than my own life. I commit the rest of my life to seeking this healing and pursuing it. I can care for my god-children and those around me from a healed place, establishing a new path for the next generation and the generations to come. My family tree has been forever changed.

This means more... For the longest, I struggled with feeling different (or set apart) from my family, often wondering if God had dropped me off at the wrong address. There was so much chaos and confusion that I was not sure I could ever see the other side of it, but I am learning that God has placed me here for such a time as this. God has placed me within this family to bring joy and peace while breaking the generational curses, cycles, and habits. The family he placed me in was intentional and not by accident. The mother he chose to birth me through was his plan all along. The lack of our relationship has propelled me to pursue God in an intense and intentional way, drawing me closer to him.

I rest in God's Word. *Although my father and mother have abandoned me, yet the Lord will take me up (adopt me as his child) (Psalm 27:10 AMP). Can a mother forget the baby at her breast and have no compassion on the child she has borne? Though she may forget, I will not forget you (Isaiah 49:15 AMP). Though my father and mother forsake me, the Lord will receive me (Psalm 27:10 NKJV). For the Lord will not reject his people, he will never forsake his inheritance (Psalm 94:14 NKJV). What then, shall we say in response to these things? If God is for us, who can be against us? (Romans 8:31 NKJV).*

These scriptures give me great comfort in knowing that where I am lacking, God fulfills. He has fulfilled me and given me several bonus moms throughout my journey in life. These women have taken me as their own daughters and loved on me like I was their own. So while my relationship with my mom is a work in progress, God has still fulfilled my needs. I am forever grateful to those who have taken me in. Which I am reminded that my God shall supply all my needs according to his riches and glory in Christ Jesus (Philippians 4:19). Jesus, be the center of it all; it is all about you!

- ❖ **Reflect on your life:** What has been your relationship with your father and mother? Did you see any correlation between how you view your parents versus how you view God? What can you positively decree and declare over your family?

CHAPTER 3

My Brother's Legacy

My older brother, Antwoyne Edwards, was an incredible human being. He was known for his energy, a great big smile, and always having "Jesus" shaved in the back of his head. When we were younger, my brother always got picked on but eventually grew muscles, increased in height, and learned how to box, so he became a man of great stature. He stood out among the crowd without even trying. He was the only boy of the children, and he was the second oldest (yep, he grew up with all the estrogen in the house). He was kind, gentle, compassionate, and loving. He was the star football player in high school, an amazing 100-meter hurdle runner, and, overall, a guy everyone loved.

When he was graduating high school, he wrote a special letter to his entire graduating class inviting them to know Jesus. He wanted everyone to come to know God in a personal way; he truly was special. When I was in junior high school, he began to allow me to work out with him. He immediately put me in the weight room to build up my strength, and we worked on agility to increase my speed and vertical jump. I am the athlete I am because of him. I watched him prepare for football games with intensity, hard work, and without slack. I never heard him make excuses but only talk of how he could improve. I worked hard because he instilled that in me.

Due to the fact my dad was a truck driver and not home during the week, I really looked up to my big brother as a father figure. He always protected me and looked out for me. He loved church and had a big heart for God. He was always studying God's Word and strived to grow closer and closer to God. When we attended church camp in the summers, he would sign up for the talent show, and one year he performed Kirk Franklin's song "Stomp" and stole the show. He had the crowd going wild and was a great performer. He would light up every room he walked into, and he left an indelible impression on everyone he encountered. I rarely saw him upset, and you could not stay angry when he was around. He always had a way of making you laugh and bringing a smile to your face. He was genuinely loved across the town, and even when he went off to college at Ouachita Baptist University in Arkadelphia, Arkansas, he was cherished. This was the brother I loved, adored, and cherished.

When I was seventeen years old (two weeks before my high school graduation), grief struck my family on April 21, 2000 in a way that changed our lives forever. The house phone rang around 6:30 a.m., and on the other end of the phone was my twenty-year-old brother's football coach. Immediately, I knew something bad had happened to my brother; my instincts said he was gone. Here is the conversation I recall:

Coach: Good morning; this is Antwoyne's football coach. Is Mr. or Mrs. Evans available?

Me: This is his younger sister. Where is my brother? What happened to him?

Coach: I'm sorry; you are a minor. I cannot tell you, but please have your parents call me as soon as possible. It's an emergency.

Me: Yes, sir, I will.

I immediately hung up the phone and began to cry. I tried calling my parents, but they were not answering. I was at home alone, confused, and my heart shattering in a million pieces. I immediately called one of my older sisters, who was away at college at the time. I was telling her about the phone call but still had no confirmation about what was happening. My mom finally came home and told me that my brother had drowned in a lake. He was gone. Initially, they could not find his body, but eventually, it surfaced in the lake.

My heart shattered and life changed forever. My family would never ever be the same (and we were not). In the blink of an eye, I experienced unspeakable pain and grief. Prior to my brother's passing, he had come home to sit with me as I signed my national letter of intent to play collegiate volleyball at Cisco Junior College. He always took me to work out with him when he came home to visit, and this last time was no different. My brother was a hardworking, Jesus-loving man of God. He was irreplaceable; you do not meet many people like that. He was his own barber and always shaved Jesus in the back of his head.

On the night of his passing, he had just made his public declaration to go into ministry. He announced he was called to preach the gospel (something he had already been living out). He was a LIGHT for others and lived a bold and courageous life. I have so many incredible memories of him, and he truly left a legacy. He was an amazing person, and I was beyond distraught to lose him. Even though he had always talked about going to live with Jesus to finally sit at his feet and worship, I still found it extremely hard to process that his life here on earth stopped at age twenty. I felt the pain of this loss for years upon years after his passing. In the earlier years, I often found myself angry and questioning God about why this had to happen to my brother. I was supposed to have more time with him. Why do bad things happen to good people?

I did not like visiting Big Spring for years after this because it was a reminder of our loss, and the pain was too much to bear. Through all the pain and my questions, I could feel God's loving arms wrapped around me, giving me comfort. He allowed me to express my pain and still loved on me. Years later, I began having dreams of my brother. A few times, I have been able to hug him and feel his presence and protection. Each time has felt so real, and it gave me great comfort in knowing he is doing just fine in heaven. In a way, I still do not understand this loss, but I find great comfort in knowing that my brother did his part for the kingdom and left a legacy on this earth. People still talk about him today and the impact he had on their lives, and this is the kind of legacy I want to leave—to know that I changed people's lives and touched their hearts for the better. He is greatly missed, but I know he is where he always wanted to be, sitting at the feet of Jesus.

This means more... we cannot control when, where, or how someone leaves this earth, but we can trust our Heavenly Father and find comfort in his Word. Once I processed and accepted his transition, I was at peace. Philippians 4:7 (NKJV) says, *And the peace of God, which surpasses all understanding, will guard your hearts and minds through Christ Jesus.* You may not always understand, but in the midst of it all, you can still find peace. God did not promise us a world free from pain and heartache, but in John 16:33 (NKJV), he says, *These things I have spoken to you, that in Me you may have peace. In the world you will have tribulation; but be of good cheer, I have overcome the world.* He has promised to *console those who mourn in Zion, to give them beauty for their ashes, the oil of joy for mourning, the garment of praise for the spirit of heaviness; that they may be called tress of righteousness, the planting of the Lord, that he may be glorified (Isaiah 61:3 NKJV).* My life has never been the same since this loss, but I proudly carry the legacy of my brother with me everywhere I go. I carry his legacy by exemplifying some of his characteristics and striving to live a life well-lived while honoring God with the gifts and talents he has given me just as my brother did.

- ❖ **Reflect on your life:** Have you lost a loved one? What has brought you comfort? How can you move forward and carry your loved one's legacy?

CHAPTER 4

Sister, Sister

My family dynamic has always been interesting and confusing. Going off to college and seeing how my friends interacted with their parents and siblings was different, a foreign concept for me. I thought how my family interacted was how every family was until God began to open my eyes and show me new things. For example, my sisters and I would go months without communicating. Being the youngest of four girls and prior to therapy, calling my sisters for advice or assistance was foreign. For over a decade, I avoided long periods of time with my family because it was a constant reminder of the chaos from childhood, the loss of my brother, and the disconnect of our relationships.

My dad frequently calls me a city girl and tells me I am not a country girl anymore, and I totally agree. I am absolutely accustomed to city life, which I have grown to love. To be honest, I also believe we all communicated less because we were dealing with our grief in our own way. As the years went on, I believe my mother ran an interference, causing even more division among us through the spreading of lies and untold truths. She manipulated and deceived others into thinking she was telling the truth and something was wrong with everyone else. As you can imagine, this was not good for a sister-to-sister relationship that already struggled from a lack of communication and misunderstanding.

When I connected with my friends from college who have turned into life-long friends and sisters, I truly began to see the power of sisterhood. I have a few amazing groups of dynamic women surrounding me who have built me up, cried with me, prayed for me, and celebrated life with me. We have simply done life together. Through the ups and the downs, these women have been there for me. One of my sister circles is my Texas Southern crew. The sport of volleyball has brought us together, along with a passion for sports in general and a love for our beloved alma mater.

My TSU crew is everything to me. They are the first place I recognized unconditional love and acceptance for all of me and my quirkiness. No matter what, these women have cheered me on. They are women of excellence; they shine in all they do. They have doctorate and master's degrees; they are mothers, sisters, daughters, wives, mentors, and the like. They make me want to be a better person and are the epitome of amazing women. They have battled health issues and won the fight. They have faced craziness at work and continue to rise up. They are professional, intelligent, fun, and easy-going. They have endured tragedy and trauma, and yet they still stand, and they have walked with me through all my "crazy" decisions. They are my tribe, my travel buddies, my sisters, and I love them dearly.

Next, I have my Toyota Center crew. I met these women selling tickets at the box office for the Toyota Center, home to the Houston Rockets. We have remained connected over the years. We laugh together, do happy hour together, and travel occasionally. This crew has kept me laughing, especially when we talk crazy to each other (in a fun way). They have always been an important part of my circle, and no matter the miles between us, we will forever be the Toyota Center crew. In 2015, we lost one of our dear crew members, Rochelle, our friend and sister. We miss her dearly and wish she was here to share in this life with us. She was my prayer partner and encourager. It has been five years since she has been gone, and I still miss her like I got the phone call that she had transitioned yesterday. We love you, Rochelle!

A host of other women have also contributed to my life, supporting me, encouraging me, and loving on me. I do not think it's a coincidence that God has always surrounded me with strong women. He has given me a heart for women to encourage and serve them. When I reflect back, I can see how I did not have the best foundation for building solid friendships, yet somehow, God still made a way to show me what it is like to have amazing women around me. I would not be any part of who I am without these women in my life. My tribe(s) know who they are, and I am forever grateful for the love, friendship, and sisterhood we share.

Over this last year particularly, as I have reflected on my relationships with my biological sisters, I had a disconnect that I wanted to bridge. I began to ask myself how I could be so connected with so many other women and not be connected to my own sisters. For years, I have circled my sisters in prayer, wondering if God would or could restore our relationship. To be honest, I reached a point where I stopped praying for that because it seemed like nothing was changing. As we all know, sometimes it feels like God is not hearing us, but that is FAR from the truth. He hears us, but we must remember, we have to do our part.

This year, when I became intentional about reaching out to my sisters more, I saw God moving in our relationship. For the first time in my entire adult life, I lived fifteen minutes from one of my sisters. I could visit her more frequently and be there when she needed help. This felt different, but good. She eventually moved out of Texas, but we had begun to communicate more and have kept that going.

I desire to bring healing to my own sisters and to interact with them like I do my other crews, but I also know this task is much bigger than what I could do on my own. So I enlisted the services of a family therapist to help us bridge the gap. I was not sure how my sisters would take this information or if they would even be interested in talking with one, but I knew I had to give it a try. Two of my sisters immediately agreed to participate, and earlier this year, we had our first sister session. My heart was overjoyed that we felt the same way about many things that have taken place in our family but have just struggled to actually sit down collectively and talk about them. For the first time, I felt hopeful and positive that we really could have a strong bond as sisters if we just put in the work. We are continuing in the family therapy sessions, and I just know this will change our family dynamic forever.

I am so glad I did not sit back and keep quiet on this. It is time out for managing chaos and living with it. It is time to heal old wounds so we can go forth in life as whole individuals and bonded as sisters. I am happy to say that after years of being distant, my sisters and me are working toward being true sisters, and I love it. For the first time in a while, one of my sisters flew to Houston, and we hung out for the weekend. We had a great time talking, eating, celebrating life, and just enjoying each other's company as sisters. And we recently had a Zoom call as a group to just connect and talk. We chatted for almost two hours, catching up on life. Amazing things can happen when the lines of communication are opened and individuals are willing to participate to make relationships better. This was the beginning of many more times of connecting and being intentional with each other.

This means more... I could have lost all hope BUT GOD had a plan all along. He was intentional about placing me around strong women to show me the power of sisterhood and connection. I understand now more than ever that we as women need each other. We do not have to compete or take away from each other, but we have enough space to exist and operate together. I thrive in my life because of the women I am surrounded by. Sisterhood has provided me a safe place for my true self to emerge. I am working to become the best version of myself because of the women who have contributed to my life. If you do your part, I promise God will show you all the benefits of what being connected to other women can and will do for your life. I am forever thankful for my sisters both by blood and by choice. Ecclesiastes 4:9-10 (NKJV) says, *Two are better than one, because they have good reward for their labor. For if they fall, one will lift up his companion. But woe to him who is alone when he falls, for he has no one to help him up.* We are not meant to do life alone. Get you a sister who can help you. You will go much further in life with the help of a friend.

❖ **Reflect on your life:** Do you have sisters or a circle of women in your life? How would you describe the dynamic of your relationship, listing all the good, bad, and ugly things? How can you do more (on your part) to improve your relationships?

CHAPTER 5

Financial Freedom

At a young age, I was introduced to credit cards as I watched my mom spend. I learned I could get what I want now and pay for it later. I thought having debt was a normal part of life. Every two weeks I was using my paycheck to pay for a plethora of bills, as many people are accustomed to doing. It was a terrible way to operate, but that is how I lived my life through college and even post-college. I found myself shopping to stay entertained, and to suppress my sadness, anxiety, and fears. I was always the friend who picked up the bill at happy hour because I had the credit limit to do so. Even though I understood math, this was not enough for me to curtail my own personal spending and money management. My dad introduced me to Dave Ramsey and his thoughts on money in my earlier years, but I had not taken it seriously. I operated the family budget when I was in junior high and high school, but I clearly did not fully understand what I was doing (the family budget is more than fun math problems to figure out). Managing money is more about your behavior and like many, I had bad behavior.

As I began to review my finances, I was seriously bound by surmounting credit card debt and a car loan. Once I read Dave Ramsey's book, *The Total Money Makeover*, I knew I had to get my life together financially. I began to see there is more to life than paying creditors and I was determined to find out what was on the other side of financial freedom. I also understood my struggle to manage my finances was a spiritual battle manifesting itself in the physical world. Once the light bulb finally went off, I found myself with severe credit card debt, and I probably owned almost ten cards (Visa, Mastercard, Discover, Macy's,

New York & Company, CareCredit—you name it, I had it) and I had a car loan. I had almost as much debt as my annual salary (let that sink in). I was making good money but struggling.

I decided to pick up extra jobs to ease some of the financial burden. There I was working as an accountant, working in the box office selling tickets to Houston Rockets games (which I did for almost seven years), and working at Chase Bank on the weekends processing checks (for one year). I was completely exhausted from this, and as you can imagine, I had no social life. I worked seven days a week, and I absolutely despised this routine but at that time, it was what I needed. I was mad at myself for putting myself in this position, but I was determined to get myself out of debt and pay every cent that I owed.

Proverbs 22:7, *The rich rules over the poor, and the borrower is slave to the lender,* was very present and active in my life, and I hated it. Racking up all this debt was so easy and almost mindless. Living an undisciplined life is costly and will make you feel helpless and hopeless, but I am here to say it will not be like this always. If you put in the work, *you can* dig your way out of the financial holes you are in.

While working my three jobs, I began the Dave Ramsey Debt Snowball. This approach helped me tremendously because I got a lot of quick wins along the way. I focused on paying off the smallest bill, paying it off as quickly as possible, and then focusing on the next bill, and so on. As I paid off the credit balances, I began to cut up the cards and close them so I could retrain how my brain thought about credit to ensure I did not continuously dig a hole rather than coming out of one. I was not concerned with my credit score; my sole focus was paying off the balances and closing the cards.

I also learned to pay cash for the simple things, like gas, groceries, and miscellaneous spending. Each pay cycle, I went to the bank and withdrew cash to cover those expenses for the month. This also retrained my brain because you typically spend less when you see cash leaving your hands. Creating a budget is critical to controlling your spending. One of my favorite Dave Ramsey quotes is, "Spend your money on paper so you can see where it is going instead of wondering where it went." Creating a budget helped me have a clear plan for how to spend my money. As with all things in life, once you define a plan, you now have a clearer path on how to achieve the goal. *Then the LORD answered me and said: "Write the vision and make it plain on tablets, that he may run who reads it (Habakkuk 2:3).*

My goal was complete financial freedom; therefore, I had to work the budget plan to achieve it. While focusing on financial goals, I also went back to school to get my master's degree in Business Administration, with an emphasis in Accounting. My employer at the time reimbursed my grad school tuition (insert praise dance). I had to take out student loans to initially pay for school, then once the semester was complete, I submitted my reimbursement form to my employer and received that pay back.

I used the tuition reimbursement to assist with paying off my credit card bills, which had a much higher interest rate. Because I was in school, I could defer any payments on student loans, so I focused solely on paying off credit cards. This had a tremendous impact because I would not have to spend years paying variable interest rates on credit cards, and my student loans were at a fixed rate. I completed grad school within eighteen months and paid off almost half of my credit cards during this time. I also received promotions at work over the years, which increased my pay.

Eventually, I had made such significant progress over the years that I patted myself on the back and became laxed. I continued with my budget but was less focused on aggressively attacking the remainder of my debt. I had begun to tell myself, *You have worked so hard; you deserve to pause and take a moment to enjoy your life and travel.* This detour lasted a few years. I did not collect more debt, but I did not aggressively pay it off either.

During this time, I also resigned from my job as an accountant. I was stressed out and not willing to endure the chaos of Corporate America, so I lost the bulk of my income for six weeks until I began consulting. I continued to make the minimum payments on my credit cards, car loan, and student loans. After almost two years of consulting, I returned to a role in accounting, which afforded me the additional financial resources I needed, and eventually I became sick and tired of being sick and tired of making payments. I worked my budget diligently and began to speak affirmations over myself (i.e. I am financially free, I give myself permission to prosper and grow, etc.). I became extremely serious in paying off the remainder of my debt and completely setting myself free. Every dollar of every paycheck was assigned to necessities (rent, food, water, gas, etc.) and paying off debt. I received monetary rewards and annual bonuses and applied all these funds to pay down balances. Note, during this time, I had to tell myself 'NO' and I did not allow myself to shop or splurge on anything unnecessary. If I could not afford to pay for it with my debit card, then I could not buy it. In May of 2018, I made my last debt payment and have remained debt free. My own journey has encouraged me to empower and assist others on their journey to financial freedom which is why I have started my own financial coaching business to be your financial champion along your journey.

This means more… This chapter of my life was sent to teach me many lessons on having order in my life. Being disciplined in my finances has impacted my life tremendously in the long term. Having financial freedom allows you to make different decisions in life than the average person. As Dave Ramsey always says, "Live like no one else now so you can live like no one else later." Now my decisions are no longer clouded by financial barriers and money, but instead, I have the freedom to choose. The biggest opportunity I have is to give more freely. I can give and support organizations of my choosing. God has called me to be a generous giver, and it is fun and fulfilling to help others. As a reminder, God has called us to be good stewards over what he has given us right where we are right now. Once I began managing my money, God continued to provide the increase. If you do your part,

God will do his! *I know what it is to be in need, and I know what it is to have plenty. I have learned the secret of being content in any and every situation, whether well fed or hungry, whether living in plenty or in want. I can do all things through him who gives me strength (Philippians 4:12-13 NKJV).*

- ❖ **Reflect on your life:** Be honest, where are you financially? Do you currently use a budget? Can you imagine how much more you can do in your life if you didn't have to pay a creditor? Are you interested in pursuing financial freedom?

CHAPTER 6

Community

Webster's dictionary defines community as the people with common interests living in a particular area; a group of people with a common characteristic or interest living together within a larger society; or a group linked by a common policy. As I have grown older, the importance of having community around me is vital. We are not meant to do life alone. I believe God has created us to be in relationship with each other, and we all desire to be loved, appreciated, and accepted by those around us. Through reflecting on the different puzzle pieces of my life, I see that I was often surrounded by community. When I wasn't, it was because I chose to isolate myself, at which time I found life a lot harder and more difficult to manage.

It is vital to be connected to the right people. We need people who will lift us up, make deposits into our life, and encourage us. We do not want to be attached to people who will bring us down and constantly withdraw from our life. Having discernment and wisdom to know those people will make or break your life. In college, I was surrounded by my coaches, teammates, and the baseball team, many of whom I am still in contact with today after twenty years. While in college, I was not only growing up and learning how to become an adult, but I was also still dealing with the loss of my brother. Having the connection with my baseball guys helped fill that brother void. I wholeheartedly believe that men and women can be just friends because I have experienced that in my life and still experience it today. I have had a strictly platonic friendship with a male roommate for nine years, and the friendship is still healthy.

When I lived in Waukegan, Illinois and Charlotte, North Carolina, I built a solid community of young professionals and Christian women around me to assist me in that season of my life. My life in Houston consists of a big community of men and women who help me navigate through life. Some are people I connected with in college, some are people from work, and some are people from church. We simply do life together (we laugh, cry, celebrate, and enjoy sharing moments together).

In China, I had an amazing group of people who were an important part of my journey. Although I was much older than most of them, having that connection with those thirteen years younger than me contributed greatly to my life. There was no way I could have gotten through that experience without their love and support. This community picked me up when I was down and homesick. They cheered me on when I was facing challenges. They loved on me when I wanted to get on the next flight back to the States. Regardless of our age differences, I am forever grateful for those connections.

I believe God is intentional about who he sends to help us along our journey in life. Each connection is purposeful and has a divine assignment. To be clear, some people are meant to be around for a lifetime, and some are only meant to be around for a season. That is why staying connected to God and discerning when someone's time is up is so important. I had some friendships during my college years that I could no longer keep later in my adult life. They served their purpose for their time, and when it was time to shift, I had to move on. There is no love lost, and I wish them all the best. Your community will evolve, grow, and change over time, but more than anything, we cannot afford to stay stagnant and within our comfort zones.

If you are in a new place and need to build community or foster new friendships, I encourage you to not be afraid to engage in conversation with those around you. Attend networking events, find an organization to join, get involved in a local church, or sign-up for community service events. You need the right community to help encourage and lift you up. Do not be afraid to surround yourself with the type of community you need to flourish and thrive in life. The only person who can determine what that looks like is you!

This means more... As I reflect on all the people who are/have been a part of my community, I am grateful for each one. Their divine assignments to me in their particular season(s) of my life have contributed to who I am today. I do not believe things happen by mere coincidence, but God has a specific purpose and plan for it all. Ecclesiastes 3:1-8,11 (NKJV) says:

> *To everything there is a season, a time for every purpose under heaven. A time to be born, and a time to die; a time to plant, and a time to pluck what is planted; a time to kill, and a time to heal; a time to break down, and a time to build up; a time to weep, and a time to laugh; a time to mourn, and a time to dance; a time to cast away stones, and a time to gather stones; a time to embrace, and a time to refrain from embracing; a time to gain, and a time to lose; a time to keep, and a time to throw away; a time to tear, and a time to sew; a time to keep silence, and a time to speak; a time to love, and a time to hate; a time of war, and a time of peace. He has made everything beautiful in its time. Also, he has put eternity in their hearts, except that no one can find out the work that God does from beginning to end.*

God has a plan and purpose for each person you have encountered in your life. Note: This should be a two-way street also; not only should you be receiving from them, but you should give as well.

- ❖ **Reflect on your life:** Who is in your community? Are they investing into your life or constantly making withdrawals? Does anyone need to make their exit out of your life? Are you doing your part to edify and encourage others in your community?

CHAPTER 7

We All Need Therapy

In 2012, I had my very first therapy session at the age of thirty years old. I found myself overweight, on high blood pressure medication, dealing with a break-up with my ex-boyfriend, stressed out at work (hence the medication), trying to manage relationships in a dysfunctional family after childhood trauma, still suppressing the emotions from the loss of my brother, and wondering what in the world was going on with my life. Suppressing all these emotions had taken its physical toll on my body. I knew there was more to life than this, and I wanted help finding it. I love Jesus, and I absolutely believe in the power of prayer, but I knew I needed more. I needed help from a professional. I no longer cared what other people would think if they knew I was in therapy or about the stigma that only those who suffer from a mental illness need it.

I reached out to my company's Employee Assistance Program (EAP) to find a counselor in my area, which provided the first two sessions at no cost to me. We successfully located someone, and I attended my first session. This was the beginning of opening my eyes to all the feelings and emotions I had learned to conceal over time and shifting my life in a new, positive direction. I sat in my first session with a Christian counselor as I cried my heart out to the point of hyper-ventilation. There was so much that I wanted to talk about and address. The priority in that moment was learning how to grieve.

I learned that over the years, I had not grieved the loss of my brother but only suppressed the emotions. I cried at the thought of losing him but had not quite accepted that my only brother had drowned in a lake at age twenty. He was my idol, my best friend, my big brother.

His sudden passing was devastating for my family and our community. For years, I had struggled with managing the emotions of this loss. Therapy gave me the tools I needed to process my grief and accept it. I began journaling my emotions and I read the book *On Grief & Grieving* by Elisabeth Kubler-Ross and David Kessler which also helped tremendously. For the first time in twelve years, I felt the weight of the world was lifted off my shoulders. I was physically breathing differently because I had finally accepted that my brother was no longer here on earth. There are still tears at times because I miss him, but I began to think about all the wonderful memories we had.

Once I moved through the grieving process, I began to address some of the other issues I had learned to cope with. Note: just like your community is important, you should also discern the right person to work with in healing. The Christian counselor served her purpose in helping me through grief; however, her religion began to cloud our sessions as we discussed other areas, and after three months I no longer felt she could assist me. Please do not get me wrong—I am a Christian woman and fully believe in the principles stated in God's Word. But in therapy, I did not want to hear religion. I was seeking truth and freedom for my real-life issues, and the therapist's "thou shalls" were not setting me free.

I stopped going to therapy for a few years, and eventually, those remaining undealt with issues showed up again in my life through a dating situationship. We were in a situation but not a relationship. I sought therapy again in 2016 to do more work in healing my life because, as we all know, relationships are mirrors. They can be a reflection of our inner being. This new therapist has been a godsend. She is Christian; however, our sessions are not filled with religious talk. She has listened to me and offered sound advice that has aided in my healing process.

Overall, therapy gives me the space I need to address the issues in my life and has helped me to become more of a happy, loving person. I love talking to someone who does not know me, and with whom I can be open and honest about everything I am feeling and experiencing.

Therapy has given me the tools I need to be emotionally and mentally healthy as I work toward the destination of wholeness in my life. So why do I think everyone needs therapy? We all have experienced trauma (or hard times) in some form. Whether you grew up in a one-parent household and your mom had to work all the time to provide—therefore she was not present—or you had a dysfunctional and chaotic two-parent household, or you were bullied as a child and now you are afraid that everyone will hurt you, or you had siblings who always took things from you and now you think everyone is here to take something away as an adult, therapy helps free your mind from old mindsets. It helps you understand yourself better and why you respond to certain situations the way you do, and it helps you process trauma and gives you the space to acknowledge your emotions and feelings through any situation.

Therapy has been life saving for me, and because of its benefits and the simple fact that sometimes life is simply hard, we can utilize the gift God has given us in therapists and counselors. Another major benefit of therapy is it will allow you to develop healthy relationships with other people. When you have done your part to go through the healing process for your own life, you are healthy and stronger for someone else. I do not believe we were designed to limp through life, suppressing our pain and coping with our emotions. To be clear, therapy is not only for when something is wrong in your life. I now use therapy as a tool to remain in a healthy state. We are meant to live a life of wholeness, and the only way to it is through the process.

This means more... Although painful, God can use our experiences for his glory. He will use our pain as a train to our purpose and destiny. Romans 8:28 (NKJV) says, *And we know that all things work together for good to those who love God, to those who are called according to his purpose.* It is bigger than what we experienced. What you experienced and learned can be used to heal someone else and set them free. Can you imagine what your life would be like if you had a healthy way to process your pain and thoughts? Galatians 5:1 (AMP) says, *It was for* *this freedom that Christ set us free [completely liberating us]; therefore keep standing firm and do not be subject again to a yoke of slavery [which you once removed]. John 8:36 (NKJV) Therefore if the Son makes you free, you shall be free indeed.* Each day, I now get to wake up and choose to live a life in freedom. Healing is a journey and I am working towards my destination of wholeness.

- ❖ **Reflect on your life:** What have you experienced in your life that has caused pain, uneasy feelings, or trauma? How can you take that pain and turn it into your purpose? How can it be used to help someone else? Will you consider finding a therapist to talk with?

CHAPTER 8

Destined to Be an Accountant

Since I was in elementary school, I have always had a love for numbers (yes, I am one of the weird ones). For my birthday, I requested number flashcards so I could get better at quickly adding, subtracting, multiplying, and dividing. Numbers challenged me and solving math problems made me feel accomplished. This came in handy when I was in the seventh grade and began to take over the family budget. Since my dad was always on the road, I had to jump in and assist. Each week, my dad and I spent his entire paycheck on paper. We allocated each dollar to the necessary categories, and I physically wrote the checks to pay the utility bills.

This became fun and intriguing for me and gave me a sense of responsibility. In high school, they offered accounting courses. I had the best teacher in Mrs. Tannehill. She taught me so much and made class incredibly fun. I enjoyed learning to record a journal entry, prepare a balance sheet, review an income statement, and reconcile bank transactions. I was excited to have homework in this class. Clearly, I was destined to be an accountant.

As you can imagine, I had no issues deciding on my college major; it was clear accounting was my route. I dreamed of being a Certified Public Accountant (CPA) and a Chief Financial Officer (CFO) of a company one day. In May 2005, I graduated from the best historically black college and university (HBCU), Texas Southern University, in Houston, Texas. I earned a Bachelor of Administration Degree (B.B.A) with a concentration in accounting. I loved learning more information about principles of accounting, accounting information systems, federal income tax, intermediate accounting, auditing, business law, and advanced accounting. I even served as president of the Jesse H. Jones School of Business chapter of Beta Alpha Psi, an international honor society for accounting, finance, and information systems students.

I was thrilled and excited to gather all this knowledge, but because of my sports schedule, I couldn't do many internships in college. In other words, I had knowledge with little real-life experience. During my senior year and before graduation, I was blessed to solidify a financial analyst position in a leadership development program for a Fortune 500 healthcare manufacturing company. This program was designed to help recent college graduates transition into the corporate world and develop the leadership skills necessary to succeed. We were required to work a rotation in an assigned department for one year and then relocate to another city (a few opportunities were open abroad as well) for a new rotation. The average time in the program was two to three years.

This fun and exciting opportunity relocated me to Gurnee, Illinois (a suburb of Chicago) shortly after graduation. I had never been to the Chicago area before, and in fact, I never even visited before accepting the job offer. I remember signing my apartment lease over a fax machine (whew, telling my age here). In July 2005, I officially made my move and began working in the Respiratory Care division in the Waukegan, Illinois office. Working hard during the accounting close period brought me joy and excitement.

After my one-year rotation was complete, I was assigned a position in Fort Mill, South Carolina at a manufacturing facility, where my workload focused on cost accounting and manufacturing processes (this was my least favorite type of accounting). I lived in Charlotte, North Carolina and commuted to South Carolina each day. I shortened my time in North Carolina to relocate back to Houston, Texas in June 2007. I then began working in the utilities industry as an accounting analyst. My work centered around financial statement analysis, preparing cash flow statements, utilizing different accounting and trading systems, and performing accounting reconciliations.

I was extremely fortunate to have great supervisors and leaders who invested in me. After one year at this company, I was promoted to senior accounting analyst. A few years later, I was then promoted to lead accounting analyst, becoming a supervisor overseeing other accountants. I was astonished at the career track I was on, and two years later at the age of thirty, I was offered a position as an accounting manager. This seemed like the natural progression for my career, and I gladly accepted. I looked forward to learning from my director and working in fixed assets (this was a completely new area for me).

This turned out to be the worst experience of my career. It was not because of the work but because of the leadership above me. I sometimes felt leadership had me on a sinking ship, not providing the support and assistance I needed as someone adapting to a new role. My career and reputation were in jeopardy, and I was underpaid and overworked. This, combined with the internal pressure I placed on myself, was unhealthy, and I began seeing the physical impact when I was diagnosed with high blood pressure. I became stressed and overburdened and began questioning whether accounting was no longer for me.

In 2013, I made one of the biggest decisions of my life; after six months in the position, I resigned and left the company. This brought a whirlwind of emotions, but after fasting and praying, I was at peace with my decision. Normally, people solidify another job before leaving the other, but I did not. I wanted to leave so badly that I was willing to take that step of faith. I continued to remind myself that my confidence and my source come from God. I did not depend on a paycheck to be my provider. For six weeks, I was able to rest and not work. God supplied all my needs during this time—all my bills were paid and I had plenty of food to eat.

After this period of rest, I accepted a new position as an accounting consultant at an oil and gas giant located in Houston's Energy Corridor. I worked there for a year and a half in a stress-free environment. I was hired to review and improve the company's account reconciliations for its pipeline business. This was second nature to me and was not challenging. I was grateful for this opportunity because it allowed me to catch my breath and get a second wind. Eventually, I needed something more challenging, as I was accustomed to a very fast-paced work environment.

In 2015, my former supervisor at the utilities company mentioned she had an open position. I jokingly said I would return if the company met my salary requirements. I was sure the company would not accept this because it was more than my salary when I initially left, and the open position was in a different department and a level down from my last role. To my surprise, they agreed to my salary requirements. God really did redeem and repay me for all that I endured. Ruth 2:12: *The Lord repay your work, and a full reward be given you by the Lord God of Israel, under whose wings you have come for refuge.*

During this time, I continued to see God's favor, and I worked there faithfully until I was laid off in 2018 due to a company merger. Upon notification of the layoffs, I was asked to serve on the transition team and was provided substantial monetary compensation. This was well beyond what I had ever seen before. Because of this compensation, I was able to achieve financial freedom. I completed the seven-month transition period and exited the company in November 2018.

To be honest, I was grateful for the layoff. This gave me the opportunity to really pursue God in a whole new way. I absolutely had moments of anxiety and worry, but I continued to remind myself that **God will keep me in perfect peace whose mind is stayed on him because I trust in him (Isaiah 26:3)**. I had to allow my faith to be louder than my fears, as I had done before in my career and my life. I had to reach back in my faith files to remind myself that just like God took care of me when I moved to the Chicago area, then North Carolina, and back to Houston, he was still capable of taking care of me now.

I was looking to take time away from life in Corporate America, so in January 2019, I planned to completely switch gears and move to

China to teach English as a second language and travel the world. The unimaginable happened, and China was placed on hold. Since I did not go to China in January, I hurriedly secured an accounting position (out of a place of fear) at an oil and gas company and worked there for two months before resigning. The journey to China resumed, and in May of 2019, I relocated. I planned to be there for one year; however, God had other plans and I returned to the United States in February 2020. I was unemployed for six months until I was offered a position in accounting with my current employer.

This means more... I believe God is intentional about everything in our lives, including our careers. He had already planned long ago for me to be an accountant. Each place, each employer was a divine appointment and assignment by God. Each place I worked has allowed me to encounter and connect with many amazing people across the world. Today, I am still connected with someone from each place, reaching all the way back to when my career first began. It has also allowed me to add an incredible amount of knowledge and skills to my life that are being used outside of the accounting world. I have applied skills I have learned when serving at church or helping others. God has orchestrated and ordained every step that I have taken. Psalm 139:16 says, *Your eyes have seen my unformed substance; and in your book were all written the days that were appointed for me, when as yet there was not one of them (even taking shape).*

Through accounting, I have been able to encourage others through my faith, pray for them in life's situations, and be an example of what faith in God looks like. My attitude toward my work is different because I am reminded that I do not work for man, but I am working unto the Lord. Colossians 3:23-24 (AMP) says, *Whatever you do [whatever your task may be], work from the soul [that is, put in your very best effort], as [something done] for the Lord and not for men, knowing [with all certainty] that it is from the Lord [not from men] that you will receive the inheritance which is your [greatest] reward. It is the Lord Christ whom you [actually] serve.*

Yes, I encountered tough situations and moments in my career, but I could not let that derail or distract me from fulfilling my assignment in each place. Yes, I have failed at some things (becoming a CPA has been a hard road that I have been on and off but will still complete soon) that made me feel not smart enough or not good enough, but I have to remember that if it was easy, then everyone would do it. I must decide to fight and push through because there is an assignment on my life and people along the path that I am supposed to help. I know I am called to the marketplace.

- **Reflect on your life:** what has your career or work journey been like? Write down every job you have ever worked and the skills you have learned. Can you see how each job has played a role in your life and who you are today? How is your attitude at work? Can your coworkers see the light of Christ in you?

CHAPTER 9

A Little Here, There, and Everywhere

I have moved around in various locations throughout my adult life, mostly driven by my career, and it has allowed me to explore a few amazing cities and make lifelong connections with others all over the world. Moving from Big Spring, Texas, attending junior college at Cisco, Texas, and then eventually landing in Houston to complete my college journey allowed me to realize more incredible possibilities exist beyond my current view. Each move and new place gave me a new level of courage and boldness and pushed me outside of my comfort zone. It was unfamiliar and uncomfortable at the beginning, but I believed I could figure it out and make the best of it. Although I was terrified to leave Texas for the very first time and move to the Chicago, Illinois area, that gigantic leap of faith further expanded my mind and opened many doors that would impact my future.

When I arrived in Illinois, I did not know anyone and was only familiar with those who I met at work. For the first few months, I only went to work and back home. I sat in my apartment, wondering why I was in this new city, feeling isolated and alone. This perspective was a recipe for depression, and I knew I was called to more than this. I had to shift my perspective and do my part to begin making connections. Through my connection with a coworker, I found a church home.

Once I began attending church, I connected with others, joined the women's ministry, and built a solid community of women who encouraged me. I hung out with coworkers—we went to Chicago Cubs baseball games, explored the city, traveled to Vegas, and played kickball. I had my circle of women who helped me to grow and covered me in prayer, and I connected with the Texas Southern Alumni Chapter in Chicago. This community was vital in helping me during this season of my life. Being away from everything I was comfortable with allowed me to see God in a different light, and this is when I began to have a true, personal one-on-one relationship with him. I began to believe what his Word says about me and that he has great plans for my life.

1 Peter 2:9 (NKJV) says, *But you are a chosen generation, a royal priesthood, a holy nation, his own special people, that you may proclaim the praises of him who called you out of darkness into his marvelous light.* I am special to God, and I was chosen by him to move to Illinois. I was chosen for the job and to be at this specific office and location and to encounter the people I came across. I am chosen, and I am his special daughter. As my time in Illinois was winding down, I began wishing I had more time there, but I was thankful for the tremendous personal and spiritual growth that had taken place. I moved away feeling like I could conquer the world and do anything I set my mind to.

After one year in Illinois, I relocated to Charlotte, North Carolina, feeling confident and bold in who I was and ready to take on this new city. Because of the lessons learned in Illinois, I immediately knew what I needed to do to survive and thrive in Charlotte. My coworker Jason helped me transition and connected me to a few young professional groups. I began attending events and networking with other professionals from the finance, information technology, and banking industries. These connections turned into friendships, and before I knew it, I had a solid community of people around me. We had dinner parties at each other's homes, enjoyed happy hours, and explored the city together. We were all recent college graduates, young professionals, and navigating through this adult life.

This was one of the best times of my life. I also found a church home to get connected within the body of Christ. I loved living in Charlotte, and I thoroughly enjoyed my community. My time in Charlotte was cut short when I decided to return to Houston after eleven months. This decision has always left me longing to go back to Charlotte and explore what I interrupted there. For years, I thought about the what-ifs. What if I hadn't left when I did? What if I hadn't begun dating my boyfriend at that time (who was back in Houston) but had been open to the opportunities in Charlotte? What if, what if, what if! But I had to move on and live with my decision of relocating back to Houston.

For the next thirteen years, I made Houston my home once again. I spent my first six years constantly working, leaving little room in my personal life and attending church when I could. My boyfriend and I broke up, and I was working three jobs to pay off debt. I knew there was more to my life than this, but I did not know what. At one point, I missed Charlotte so much that I attempted to move back, but God blocked it and graced me through my terrible decisions.

After talking with a life coach, I decided to settle down and embrace what God had for me in Houston. I became more intentional with my community and church. I resigned from having multiple jobs and worked only one. This created time and space in my schedule to invest in the people and events that brought me joy. I became active in supporting my HBCU in various sporting events (yes, I am a season ticket holder), attending dinner parties, happy hours, and gatherings with friends, and I became a Sunday School teacher for the youth and served in the women's ministry at my church.

As I transitioned to a new church, I developed another circle of individuals who helped me to grow even more spiritually. I joined a Freedom group and found a new sense of purpose for my life. The group was created to walk with you through the Freedom curriculum, a thirteen-week course designed to help you live the abundant and victorious life that Christ has meant for you. It helped me embrace the truth of God's Word as it relates to how I see the world, my past, my personal value to God, and my purpose for his Kingdom. I walked through this curriculum with a small group of women, with each of us being open, honest, vulnerable, and transparent about our life experiences. After going through this process and being transformed, the next semester, I co-led a group of women through their Freedom journey. This was an extraordinary opportunity for me to invest in someone else's spiritual growth and assist them in seeing their value in Christ. Each week we diligently met, discussed the curriculum, talked about life, and prayed for each other. It was a wonderful time of connecting and impacting each other's lives.

Upon completion of the curriculum, I set off to live in Shanghai, China. I would not have had the courage to make this move without the experience of moving to various cities. The same God who kept me when I moved to Chicago and Charlotte and then back to Houston was the same God who would keep me in China. I embarked on this journey, and no matter what country I was in, I learned the same lesson, building the right community around me would be vital to my success in China. Being thousands and thousands of miles away from everything I had known and being in a country where I do not speak or write the language proved to be one of the biggest challenges of my life.

Similar to my initial move to Chicago, I spent the first few months in culture shock. I began to wonder if I had made a bad decision for my life. I shed plenty of tears and had tantrums like a little child. I eventually began to shift my perspective because I was tired of being sad every day, and I had to remind myself that even in this country, God still had a specific reason and plan for me to be here. My community consisted of my coworkers, who were fellow international teachers having the same experience as me. We connected, encouraged each other, always had dinner together, and traveled the world. There is absolutely no way that I survived my China experience without them.

My roommate and I had Jesus and wine nights. We watched church online, drank wine, and discussed the sermon and/or our life experiences. These moments brought me peace and joy and showed me that I was meant to be here for such a time as this. One day while I was having a parent-teacher conference, the advisor was working as my translator between the parents and myself. I had a vision of going to places where I did not speak the language and using a translator to proclaim the goodness of God and who he is. This encouraged me tremendously, and I knew my journey to China was not in vain.

A few months later, I abruptly headed back to the United States due to the start of the global pandemic. This time, I was unsure of what was next, but I had confidence that God would lead the way. I landed in Dallas, Texas after visiting family and felt a nudge in my spirit to stay there. I told God I would stay in this place until he moved me. I parked in Dallas, going from hotel to hotel (because I desperately wanted my own space) and eventually moving in with my cousin and his family. I expected to be at my cousin's house for approximately two weeks at most. Little did I know that the global pandemic would hit the States extremely hard and I would end up residing in Dallas for six months during quarantine.

I had moments where I wrestled with God. It felt like my life did not make sense anymore. Why would he have me give up everything I owned to move to China for nine months? I completely trusted him, and now I was feeling uncomfortable and unsettled during this transition. During the six months, I applied for job after job. I was continuously denied again and again. I wondered if God had forgotten about me. I prayed and asked God to reveal what I was supposed to learn during this season and what he wanted me to focus on at that time. He spoke the word "serve."

So instead of despising the situation, I began to serve others. I served my cousin and his family by cleaning the home and helping my cousin-in-law with groceries and around the house. Through this, I learned how I want to manage my own home one day. I served at church by calling members to check on them and praying for them while assisting with running the Facebook page during service. This allowed me to shift my focus to others and their needs to encourage them. I served friends through various life situations, which allowed us to deepen our connection. I spent time in devotion with God around 5 a.m. each morning. I read books, prayed, and fasted, which allowed me to release pride, grow spiritually, and have the words to encourage someone else.

And for the first time in my life, I started to reconnect with my sisters. We were communicating more, and because I lived in Dallas, I saw them more often. Quarantine was not a wasted season for me but rather one of enrichment and enhancement. I have a new appreciation for life because of it. During this entire time of life in Dallas, I did not have an income, but I never missed any meals. All my bills were paid and never late, and I was able to give a monetary gift each month to help cover expenses at the house. I still lived in abundance, and it was only by the grace of God. Eventually, I secured a position back in Houston, where I currently reside and work.

This means more... Each city and each country represent numerous puzzle pieces in my life. Each move gave me new levels of faith, which allowed my confidence in Christ to grow. He used each moment of transition to stretch, refine, and take me through a purification process. I would not be the woman I am today without these experiences. Fighting through the fears and uncertainty has been worth the journey. In each move, God has shown up and supplied all my needs. His word in Philippians 4:19 says, *My God shall supply all my needs according to his riches and glory by Christ Jesus*. In each place, he had a community of individuals assigned to assist me in my journey. He had provision already established. I just had to trust him through the process each time. It was uncomfortable and rough at times, but those times shaped and molded me.

- ❖ **Reflect on your life:** Have you ever moved away from family and friends? How was your experience? What did you learn during that time? Are you willing to step outside of your comfort zone?

CHAPTER 10
Relationships

As we all know, a loving relationship is the average person's biggest desire. We all want that one person to love us unconditionally, provide us with companionship, and enjoy life with. I have always been a late bloomer compared to the average person when it comes to dating relationships. I did not have my first boyfriend until college. It just was not something I focused on. In my younger years, my dad heavily instilled in me that I should not date or be worried about boys and that I needed to focus on my education above all. I took that very literally. Sure, I thought some guys were cute, but I was not actually interested in pursuing a relationship with them.

As I got older, I also understood the dynamic of my parents' relationship had impacted me a lot more than I realized. I remember my parents having a loving relationship in my younger years, and then at some point, there was a shift in the opposite direction. Home was filled with a lot of yelling and arguing. When I asked my mother why she divorced my dad after twenty years together, she stated she was never happy. She was only waiting until her children were out of the house. This baffled me, and to be honest, I still do not understand why someone would stay in an unhappy situation if they were that miserable for so long. At the same time, I continued to watch her call on my dad and depend on him financially, and my dad obliged her.

I also asked my dad, "Why do you continue to take care of someone who left you?"

He replied, "Because she is the mother of my children and I am responsible for taking care of her."

"I do not understand this either," I said. "This does not make sense to me. Why are you responsible for someone who does not want to be with you?"

This was another time when I began to look at my mother differently. In my mind, she was using my dad for financial gain, and I was determined never to depend on a man for anything because I did not want to be like that. At the same time, my dad was constantly raising me to be an independent woman who did not need to ask anyone for anything. In one conversation, he specifically told me, "You better not ask anyone for anything in this world. If you cannot go get it yourself, then you do not need it." Therefore, I learned to either make it happen for myself or do without it. I took this very literally in my life and as an adult, which is why I struggled with asking anyone for help. I was so used to doing everything on my own or figuring out solutions to problems that I did not know how to communicate to someone that I needed help. As you can imagine, this had a negative impact on me in my adult years.

As I was developing friendships and relationships, I became the person who always gave. I gave and gave and gave, never needing anything from anyone else, although this was only a façade. I did/do need help; I did/do need others, but I did not know how to communicate this. So in my late twenties, early thirties, I started to unlearn some of the behaviors that I was accustomed to. I had to make a conscious effort to ask for help, and I had to learn that asking for help did not make me weaker as a strong, independent woman, but I actually was stronger. Trying to do it all in life was a lonely place. I was often tired, exhausted, and left wondering how I was there for everyone else but could never let anyone be there for me.

I placed these unnecessary expectations on myself as a sister, friend, teammate, and coworker, but I have learned there is strength in numbers. Walking through life with a friend, knowing I have love and support, has been a beautiful thing. I feel loved, encouraged, and inspired because

I now allow those things in my life. Over the years, I have dated occasionally (but still well below the average person). Because of my parents' dynamic, I told myself I didn't want that for myself. To this day, I do not do relationships with yelling. This is a trigger for me, and I will run in the opposite direction if this begins.

Post-college and the years beyond, I was bound to an individual (let's call him guy A) and not quite sure how to break this cycle with him (it definitely was a soul tie). We connected as great friends in college, and then post-college, we crossed the friendship boundary. After that, we did not speak for almost six years because of a conversation that went completely wrong. We eventually reconnected through a mutual friend several years later. I eventually understood that we were bound by some of our trauma related to family issues, and we thought similarly in some areas. I was able to release him and move on only after I discovered some devastating information.

Then there was the five-year relationship with guy B (which occurred during the six-year period when I was not talking to guy A). I knew from the beginning that I should not have been in this relationship. Yet I continued in it, hoping to feel otherwise—always feeling the need to give, give, give and help rescue or fix someone. Do not get me wrong—I truly did care for these guys, but I was with them from a place of brokenness, not as a healthy, whole individual, and this was not the best for any of us.

Unhealthy toxic relationships seemed like the norm, and I could not see myself participating in them, so I have stayed to myself, which is overcorrecting what I experienced. Since then, I have worked with my therapist to begin healing from these broken relationships and damaged places in my life. I have learned that although I tried to run from my parents' brokenness, I eventually still chose those types of connections. I was inherently attracted to them without any effort, and now I am aware of the pattern and make the conscious effort to choose better for myself. I am doing my work to heal, and my next relationship will come from a place of wholeness rather than brokenness.

I have also learned that saying no is okay. I do not have to say yes to a guy just because he asked me out, especially when I see red flags. When I cross paths with a guy, I usually pray immediately about him and God usually provides an answer fairly quickly each time. I am still single, so I have not met the guy to say yes to, but I believe he is coming. My thoughts on marriage have shifted significantly. At the age of thirty-seven, I finally began to truly pray about marriage. As I desire a loving and healthy romantic relationship in my life, how I show up in the relationship is going to matter. Thankfully, I am healing this part of my life and unlearning the behaviors I practiced previously, but this has not been an easy journey. I have learned some hard lessons along the way.

This means more… examining where I first learned about relationships and how to engage in them has helped me bridge the gap on understanding how I show up in relationships today. Each type of relationship I have encountered (dating, friendships, family) is a puzzle piece to my life. We have to do the necessary work to release the unhealthy patterns and begin to build the loving and healthy relationships we desire. But if I go back in time, my very first relationship is that with Christ. *Romans 5:8, But God demonstrates his own love for us in this: while we were still sinners, Christ died for us; 1 John 4:9-1 reads: this is how God showed his love among us; He sent his one and only Son into the world that we might live through him. This is love: not that we loved God, but that he loved us and sent his Son as an atoning sacrifice for our sins. Dear friends, since God loved us, we also ought to love one another.* Because I have Christ as my foundation, I can now show up in relationships differently. God's love for me gives me the opportunity to then turn and love others. Sidenote: I know 'loving' other humans is not realistically the easiest thing to do at times, but this does give us a goal to work towards. We are required by God to do so.

❖ **Reflect on your life:** Where did you first learn about relationships? What did that relationship or situation show you? How do you show up in relationships now? Identify healthy and unhealthy relationships in your life. What do you believe about God's love for you? I encourage you to seek God and read about his love for you in his word.

CHAPTER 11

The Athlete

I began playing sports in middle school. I played volleyball, basketball, and ran track. I quickly learned track was not for me and gladly gave it up. I continued to play volleyball and basketball in junior high and high school. Sports was my outlet to get away from the chaos, and I saw it as a ticket to my future. Right after my sophomore year of high school, I decided to quit the basketball team and focus solely on my volleyball skills. Being the youngest of five children, I knew my parents paying for college was not an option, so my ticket out of Big Spring, Texas rested in my volleyball skills. My high school coach was not very fond of this decision, and I remember being called to the school counselor's office to discuss my decision. Thankfully, I remained firm and discontinued playing basketball.

In the spring semester of my senior year, I was offered a scholarship to a college in Pulaski, Tennessee but was not ready to be that far away from home. I later tried out for the volleyball team at Cisco Junior College in Cisco, Texas. I made the team and was offered a two-year, full-ride scholarship. I gladly accepted and signed my national letter of intent. Upon graduation, I moved to Cisco and prepared for volleyball camp.

The campus was in a small town and full of athletes. We had football, men's and women's basketball, women's soccer, softball, volleyball, and rodeo. Most of the athletes were from Dallas, Houston, or San Antonio, with a few being from New Jersey. Since it was a small town, all of us hung out together and lived the college life. I will spare you the details on the kind of fun we had, but we had a great time. As I was preparing to graduate with my Associate of Arts Degree, I began to search for a college to complete my volleyball career and obtain my bachelor's degree. I tried out at Southeastern Oklahoma State University in Durant, Oklahoma. I made the team and was offered a partial scholarship; however, because it was not a full scholarship, I declined the offer.

My former teammate, and best friend, was playing at Texas Southern University (TSU). She told the coach about my roommate and me. I submitted game film (via a VHS recording... that is how old I am, ha), and we were invited to go on a recruiting trip. We drove down to Houston and were mesmerized by the big city and big lights; we instantly fell in love. We had an amazing time on the recruiting trip, and when we returned, we both were offered full scholarships to attend Texas Southern. We happily accepted and signed our national letter of intent.

Upon graduating from Cisco, we made our way down to Houston, Texas. Excited to embrace this new city, we began volleyball practice. We did not have many wins, but I had the time of my life at Texas Southern. I thought junior college was fun, but my time at TSU was even better. I played on the team for two years, and after that, I became a student assistant for the team for one year. As I reflected on my time as an athlete, playing sports taught me important life skills and lessons that developed me into a well-rounded individual. Sports developed my skills in resilience, accountability, leadership, respect, and patience, just to name a few. I learned to manage a room full of people with different personalities, the importance of teamwork and collaboration with others, discipline I would need to be successful beyond the court, and tenacity through failures and setbacks. I never missed a single college or high school game due to injury because, despite how I felt, I was determined to show up for my teammates and play the game I loved (thankfully, I only encountered minor injuries throughout my time).

I graduated with my bachelor's degree, and this was the end of my collegiate volleyball career. I eventually played club volleyball in an adult league with other Texas Southern volleyball alumni and friends. We were team Full Force, spending all day on Saturdays playing the game we loved. We played for a few years and returned to Texas Southern to play in the annual alumni volleyball game—the current players vs. former players.

One year at the alumni game, I went up for a block and came down wrong. I landed with my ankle bent and immediately fell to the ground and cried for help. I suffered a horrible high ankle sprain. I knew then it was time to hang up my volleyball shoes for good. I gladly hung up my shoes and knee pads and have not returned to the court since (by the way, my ankle is still messed up today because I did not rehab it or complete physical therapy). In 2013, I began CrossFit. This intense exercise awakened the athlete in me once again. I was addicted to CrossFit, often working out four to five days a week. I loved lifting weights, completing wallballs, and hearing the barbells hit the ground was music to my ears. I hated the running portion, and I could never achieve a pull-up, but these weaknesses challenged me. I felt accomplished after a workout, and I loved the community of people I exercised with. I felt healthy, strong, and the most physically fit I had been since college.

This high lasted for a year and a half until I started having aggravating knee pain. After going to the doctor and having x-rays done, it was determined I did not have much cartilage left in my knee. I was grinding bone-to-bone, and the doctor stated CrossFit was no longer a viable option for me. I was in my early thirties, but I had the knees of someone in their fifties. I was devastated and cried after hearing this news. CrossFit had been my outlet, my stress reliever, and brought me joy. I was sad and depressed for a while after giving it up. This was my first serious injury as an athlete, and I did not handle it well. I mentally struggled with this injury.

A few years went by, and I decided to give this exercise thing a try once again. I joined a gym and hired a personal trainer to assist me. We worked out twice a week and were making progress. One Saturday, I went to hot yoga, and as we were in the running man pose, my knee immediately began to fill up with fluid and become swollen. I limped my way to the car and made a doctor's appointment, this time needing an MRI. The MRI confirmed I had torn my meniscus, loose cartilage was floating around, I had a baker's cyst behind my knee, and I was bone-to-bone in some areas. This required arthroscopic surgery, and in August 2016, I had my first knee procedure. This left me frustrated, sad, and feeling hopeless.

I have now vowed to start loving myself and the skin I am in, regardless of how often I can workout or what size I wear. This was important for me because I had to begin loving myself right where I was. I could not wait until I was a size two or could run five miles to start. I did some inner reflection, meditated on God's Word, and my self-esteem increased. Genesis 1:27 says, *So God created man in his own image, in the image of God he created him; male and female he created them.* I Samuel 16:7 also says, *But the Lord said to Samuel, "Do not look on his appearance or on the height of his stature, because I have rejected him. For the LORD sees not as man sees, man looks on the outward appearance, but the Lord looks on the heart."*

I do not have to be a size two in order to achieve God's plan for my life. I am not defined by the number on the scale but I can do my part by making healthier food choices and exercising. While I am working to drop the pounds, I am learning to love myself deeper each day and allow that to be my focus. The athlete is still inside of me. I just have to modify what I have always done to support my physical health and knees.

This means more… The journey of playing sports and enduring injuries is bigger than the game or the injury. Both have contributed to the development of my character and added significant value to my life. The lens through which I see life was shaped through all the highs and lows of being an athlete. There are times when you must pull more weight than someone else and times when you will have help carrying your weight. God's Word reminds us in Matthew 18:19-20 that *again, truly I tell you that if two of you on earth agree about anything they ask for, it will be done for them by my Father in heaven. For where two or three gather in my name, there am I with them.* It is better to go together rather than to go alone. Teamwork makes the dream work!

❖ **Reflect on your life:** Have you played sports or been part of a team? What characteristics were developed through this experience? What lessons did you learn? How can you apply those lessons to your everyday life?

CHAPTER 12

My HBCU Experience

Hail, Hail, Hail! to Texas Southern. Hail to our dear Maroon and Gray. Undivided we will stand. By the greatest in the land, T-S-U, T-S-U, we love you. All roads lead to Texas Southern, paved with light for one and all. T-S-U's a shining star and we are proud of what you are—T-S-U, T-S-U, we love you. I am a proud product of the best historically black college and university (HBCU) I know, Texas Southern University, also known as TSU. We have notable alumni such as Michael Strahan, Yolanda Adams, Barbara Jordan, and Kirk Whalum.

TSU was established as The Colored Junior College in 1927 to provide an opportunity for African Americans to receive college training. In 1951, the university changed its name to Texas Southern University. We currently have approximately 1,000 faculty and more than 9,500 students of different ethnic and culturally diverse backgrounds (Texas Southern History, 2020). Texas Southern took a chance on me and gave me the opportunity to further my college education. Receiving a scholarship to play volleyball and learn in the Jesse H. Jones School of Business enriched my life tremendously. Although being surrounded mostly by people who looked like me came as a culture shock, I was happy and excited, and I instantly felt at home.

Initially, I did not know much about my own culture because I grew up with predominantly white people, and I had little to no exposure to black history. When I attended TSU, I was exposed to my culture in new and enlightening ways. My professors were personable, and I felt cared for. My coaches and teammates became family and looked out for me. I met many people from all over the country with diverse backgrounds, who I am still connected to today.

Being on the yard felt like one big family reunion, with a DJ playing music in the courtyard every Friday. The overall atmosphere and environment were amazing, and I received a well-rounded experience. It also played a crucial role in shaping my identity, accepting my brown skin, and provided a level of comfort that I was around other African Americans. Honestly, I felt my presence mattered. For once, I could be in a room with people who looked like me and I did not stick out. The volleyball staff (my now TSU crew) loved the game of volleyball but reminded us we were students before we were athletes; thus, academics was a high priority.

Our university motto was "Excellence in Achievement." We were expected to do things the right way and do them well while achieving our goals and nothing less. Although volleyball was my ticket to college, I knew my career would come to an end after four years, so I remained vigilant in my studies. The Jesse H. Jones School of Business equipped me with the tools I needed to be successful in the business world. It gave me a solid education in understanding business and accounting, prepared me for interviews, and offered corporate involvement. It was also housed in a state-of-the-art facility, which created an environment for me to succeed academically.

Once I began playing volleyball, I knew I was connected to people who would be lifelong friends. Through the coaching staff and my teammates, I was surrounded by women who loved the game of volleyball like me, loved to laugh and make jokes, and have a good time. We traveled on the bus, watched movies together, and went to all the fraternity parties. We had the best time. I am forever indebted to Texas Southern because of what they provided for my life. I could not have known that I was stepping onto a campus that would change my life forever, but I am so glad I did.

Since graduating from TSU with a B.B.A. with a concentration in accounting, I have strived to remain a supportive alumna. I am an active season ticket holder, frequently attending sporting events, and a financial supporter of the university. I feel the need to give back to my alma mater so they can continue to provide an excellent experience for other students who will have a positive life-changing experience.

This means more... I believe my attendance at Texas Southern was a divine appointment by God. He had already orchestrated and ordained this plan for me long ago. My experiences and human connections were divine assignments. I gladly contribute part of who I am to TSU. This means more because this experience further opened my eyes to see the world in a different way. Experiencing the city of Houston and college allowed me to see the dopeness of my culture and I learned I can adapt to all rooms I walk into.

- ❖ **Reflect on your life:** Did you attend college? What was your college experience like? What environments have you experienced that have contributed to how you see the world? Are you open to new experiences?

CHAPTER 13

Travel, Travel, Travel

As far as I can remember, I have always had the urge to travel and explore different cultures. This is interesting because we never traveled much when I was younger. At the most, we went to family reunions in East Texas. I believe my urge to see the world comes from my dad being a truck driver for thirty-plus years. He has been to several different states (although not out of the country). When I became older, I began to see different pictures of destinations and scenery and thought, *One day I will go see this place.* I definitely had a tug in my heart to go see the world. God created all this beautiful land, and one of my life goals before I leave this earth is to step foot in all 195 countries in the world.

I grew up in a small country town, so I had never even taken a flight anywhere, but I believed there was more to the world than I had known and seen. My first flight was on September 11, 2002, when my volleyball team (Texas Southern University) was heading to play in a tournament at North Carolina A&T University. I was a nervous wreck, especially considering this was the anniversary of the horrific day we, in the United States, know as September 11, 2001 (my thoughts and prayers go out to all the families impacted by that tragic day).

I recall sitting on the flight and flowing between excitement and pure fear, praying that we would just get to our destination safely. I am happy to report that we arrived and returned safely, and I am still here to write about it. After this flight, I began to travel domestically within the United States. My next flight was for a job interview in Columbus, Ohio during my senior year of college. At this point, I was excited to take a flight and step foot in another city within the U.S.

This was only the beginning of my journey, as I have flown to various states since then—Chicago, Illinois; Las Vegas, Nevada; Charlotte, North Carolina; Dallas, Texas; Austin, Texas; San Diego, California; Sacramento, California; New Orleans, Louisiana; St. Louis, Missouri; Fort Lauderdale, Florida; Denver, Colorado; Santa Fe, New Mexico; Phoenix, Arizona; and Honolulu, Hawaii. This truly is not even a tip of the iceberg considering the U.S. has fifty states.

My first international experience came on a trip to La Romana, Dominican Republic in 2011, which was a very interesting trip. My original five-day vacation turned into a twelve-day vacation after Hurricane Irene canceled my return flight to the States, but let me not digress. This was a crazy experience that did not hinder me from traveling internationally but only excited me more. When you travel, it begins to expand your mind beyond your comfort zone. You have the opportunity to see things you would have never seen before, and it inspired a sensation within me to seek new and unknown experiences.

Although I have traveled to the Dominican Republic and Mexico, I still did not consider this true international travel, as I wanted to do more. In 2018, Juliette Bush, founder of Brave By Faith Travel, was hosting a women's travel group to Cape Town, South Africa. Inspired and intrigued, I signed up to participate. I was overwhelmed with excitement and joy as I paid for this trip, although nervous about the almost thirty-three hours of travel time (with the longest leg being a sixteen-hour flight from Houston to Dubai, then an eight-hour layover, with another nine-hour flight from Dubai to Cape Town). This initial flight seemed forever, especially because I was traveling solo and did not know any of the other women attending this experience. I embarked on the journey, a hot mess emotionally and physically but willing to press through to see what was on the other side.

I arrived in Cape Town exhausted and drained, but once I met the other women, I began to relax. I was no longer just the crazy one who would travel across the world and explore South Africa, but I was surrounded by a group of women who were just as bold as I was. This trip was a significant turning point in my life. My eyes and mind were opened to another set of possibilities and opportunities that existed for me. We spent the week partnering with Hillsong Church to learn and grow in our Christian walk, serving the Gugulethu community, climbing Lion's Head Mountain, and growing together as a group.

Each night, we were partnered with different women in the group to pray together and connect. The connections with the other women were incredible, many of who I still connect with today. Having the opportunity to hear each other's stories and pray with each other was truly a blessing. Once I returned from Cape Town, I felt inspired and encouraged that I could do anything I set my mind to, no matter what it was.

During this time, I was also informed by my employer that the company was undergoing a merger, and as a result, layoffs occurred. I interviewed for a position with the new company and was extended an offer but prayerfully declined. That meant I needed to seek God for my next opportunity. For months, I dealt with anxiety and was unclear about what my future held. I must admit, living in the unknown was terrifying for a while. To be honest, I was speaking that I trusted God, but deep down in my heart, I was afraid because of the uncertainty.

I prayerfully began to consider what international opportunities existed and thus began my research. I came across a job ad on Instagram to teach English as a second language in China. I browsed through the company's website and was very attracted by the offer to live abroad, work (and get paid), have health insurance, have the opportunity to travel the world, and no prior teaching experience was required. I immediately completed the employment application. One day later, I was contacted by a recruiter in the Shanghai office and began the interview process.

Within two weeks of applying, I had accepted a job offer and began the visa process. I had a lot of steps to complete to prepare to legally work in China. I first had to obtain a police clearance letter from my local police department, complete the 120-hour TEFL certification, send passport photos, and have all these documents notarized and authenticated by the Secretary of State in Texas to certify they were factual and true. Upon certification of these documents, then the company could begin to apply for my work visa in China. There were several trips back and forth to the Chinese Consulate office, and thankfully, I lived fifteen minutes from the Houston location. The Chinese Consulate at that time only had five locations in the United States, so I was destined to do this. The process overall was fairly smooth and easy, which is the opposite of what many people experience. This confirmed that this was exactly what I was supposed to be doing. By November 2018, I received my official work permit letter and set a start date of January 16, 2019. This is the day I was expected to arrive in China and begin work. I booked my flight and began my countdown to this major transition.

Later in the year, I participated in another Brave by Faith travel experience. This time, Jules was leading a group of women to walk where Jesus walked in Israel. This was an incredible experience. We visited Tel-Aviv, Nazareth, and Bethlehem, just to name a few locations. We set sail on the Sea of Galilee, prayed at the Wailing Wall, visited Mount Carmel and the Church of the Beatitudes, and walked through Nazareth Village. This is nowhere near a comprehensive list of the activities we participated in, but if you ever have the opportunity to join a travel experience with Brave by Faith Travel, you will not be disappointed.

On day two of the experience, we visited Caesarea Philippi and I saw a fig tree planted next to a river of water connected to the Jordan River. The scripture Psalm 1:3 came to life in a real and tangible way. It says, *He shall be like a tree planted by the rivers of water, that brings forth its fruit in its season. Whose leaf also shall not wither; and whatever he does shall prosper* (NKJV). I noticed the fig tree connected to the river of water was blossoming and full of life. Then across the walkway was a second tree not connected to the water, and it was withered and pale looking. This reminded me that is exactly how we are in real life. As we are connected to God and his Word, then we are fruitful and full of life, but when we are disconnected from him, we become withered and tired. John 15:5-6 (NKJV) says: *I am the vine; you are the branches.*

If you remain in me and I in you, you will bear much fruit; apart from me you can do nothing. If you do not remain in me, you are like a branch that is thrown away and withers; such branches are picked up, thrown into the fire, and burned. Travel truly has impacted my life in many positive ways.

This means more… We never know what situations or experiences God will use to open our minds to the endless possibilities he has for us. Experiencing travel has broadened my perspective on life and has allowed me to trust God in a deeper way. And because his word is the same yesterday, today, and forevermore, I can find confidence in knowing that he will keep me in perfect peace whose mind is stayed on him because I trust in him. As we follow God and his lead for our lives, we can live through moments of uncertainty and life in the unknown, regardless of what city or country we step into. Trust me, his plan for you is greater than you could ever imagine.

❖ **Reflect on your life:** Have you ever traveled before? Did your experience open your mind to new possibilities? In what ways were you impacted?

CHAPTER 14

Crazy Faith

In November of 2018, I completed my last day with my employer after serving on the transition team for the new company. Happy and excited, I began to pack up my apartment and prepare for my move to Shanghai, China. I had crazy faith to believe that the same God here with me in the United States would also be with me in China. I enjoyed a solid two months of no work before I was set to move. Everything was moving smoothly, and as January approached, excitement and anxiety began to creep in. I celebrated my move with family and friends and had a going-away party the Friday before I was set to take off. I was scheduled to arrive in China on January 16, 2019. We partied and celebrated, having a grand time.

On the Sunday following my party, I received a phone call that changed everything. My godson, who was two-and-a-half months old at the time, became very ill. He was taken to the emergency room in San Antonio, Texas and it was determined he had a heart defect and needed open heart surgery. As my best friend and I stood in shock and in tears, I began to contemplate what to do. Should I get on the plane and go to China in the midst of this situation, or should I stay and support those I cared about during this time? This was a heavy decision for me. Everything I had worked toward was in China, but I could not leave the United States with the baby fighting for his life and the family in disarray.

As my best friend and I drove to San Antonio the next morning, I contacted my recruiter to keep her abreast of the situation and communicated that this could delay my arrival in China. Seeing the baby in the ICU unit, connected to all the machines and tubes running from his little body, lying helpless, I knew I would struggle to leave under these conditions. I was not sure what repercussions not going to China would have on my job, but the baby's situation was more important to me. I informed the recruiter that I would not be arriving in China as we anticipated.

Not going to China also threw me into a whirlwind of more anxiety and walking into the unknown. I wondered what this decision meant and what I would do now. I had been out of work for two months now and didn't know how I would continue to survive financially. Interestingly enough, I immediately began to receive job opportunities in accounting again, which made me wonder if I was ever truly meant to go to China in the first place. Maybe I heard God wrong and this was just his way of saying he had something else in mind for me. I thought it was a test and I must have passed, so he was saving me from going.

I felt uncertain and like everything was falling apart. I did not know what to do. I wanted to make the right decisions with no regrets. I informed the recruiter that my new arrival date was February 12, 2019. However, I later had to change this again because we learned the baby would not have his open heart surgery until April 2019 (and I was not leaving the States before his surgery). I always kept the lines of communication open in hopes that if I did decide to go then, they would have me. In reality, I had a serious tug of war going on in my heart. I strongly felt like God was sending me to China, but the situation with my god baby made me feel like maybe he had changed his mind.

The thought of going back to accounting at the time gave me mixed emotions. Accounting was all I had known and was a great resource, but I was burned out, exhausted, and over it. Even still, I contemplated entertaining the job opportunities, and when I received word that the baby would not have his open heart surgery until he was a few months older, I was sure I was meant to begin applying for jobs. I interviewed and received a job offer from an oil and gas company here in Houston, which provided great opportunities, amazing benefits, and compensation package. Not just anyone could get into this company. I felt grateful and blessed to have this opportunity, so I accepted the job offer and began work on February 25, 2019.

Over the next few weeks as I began work, I continued to consider China (unknowingly to my current employer). My work visa for China expired; therefore, I had to start the paperwork process all over again. I worked to get my documents notarized and authenticated, then sent over to the Shanghai office to apply for a second work visa. I was still undecided on staying vs. going but wanted to continue the process just in case. After completing the paperwork, I received my second work visa set to expire on July 22, 2019.

People continued to ask me what I was going to do, and I had to quickly become comfortable with telling them I didn't know. This was new for me, as I have always had an answer when it comes to my life. I always had it all figured out (or at least so I thought) with a plan A, B, and C waiting in the wings. I am a forward thinker and typically can anticipate things before they happen, and I usually make decisions based on the outcome I want, but for the first time in my life, I was unsure and did not know. In the book, *The Circle Maker*, Mark Batterson writes, "It's at this place where God wants us to do something unprecedented that many of us get stuck spiritually. Instead of operating by faith, we switch back to our default setting of logic. Instead of embracing the new move of God, we fall back into the rut of our old routines" (Batterson, 2016).

This tug-of-war continued in my heart and mind for months as I was fighting faith vs. logic. Amid all this, I had a conversation with a trusted counselor at that time. She had been praying with me and supported me while I prepared for my move, and I will never forget the words she spoke to me. She reminded me that I did not know what was tied to my obedience, and God was clear that I was to go to China. Then she asked had he spoken something different to me? I was slow to speak and hesitated to answer because I knew he had not. She checked me in the most graceful and loving way and held me accountable.

I was doing great in my new role at work and was excelling in my new environment. The hours I was working reminded me of everything

I said I did not want, but I continued to press on because this was the life of an accountant that I had always known. One day, while sitting at my desk, I heard a gentle whisper say, "You are not supposed to be here." The whisper was very clear and precise. I had no doubt in my mind that God was speaking directly to me. I knew in that very moment that I needed to resign from this position and go to China. I was initially afraid to inform my employer of my decision, but I had enough confidence in what I heard God say that in the next few days, I turned in my resignation. I was willing to risk it all because I wanted to be obedient to God more than anything. I spoke to my supervisor and director and thanked them for the incredible opportunity. They were shocked but excited that I would take this giant leap of faith to go across the world to explore China.

My last day was scheduled for May 3, 2019, and I was set to arrive in China on May 7, 2019. The days leading up to my departure were emotionally tough. Everyone (including myself) thought I was absolutely insane for leaving everything I had known to embark on this journey further into the unknown. As my best friend was driving me to the airport, we tried our best to fight our tears. We dropped off my bags at the check-in, and with tears streaming down our faces (enough to fill a few buckets), I hugged her goodbye, not knowing if or when I would ever see her again. I walked through the TSA security process feeling crazy, anxious, but excited for the journey ahead.

This means more... This situation taught me so much. We have the power to choose in our lives. Deuteronomy 30:19 (NKJV) reads: *I call heaven and earth as witnesses today against you, that I have set before you life and death, blessing and cursing; therefore choose life, that both you and your descendants may live.* God gives us the choice, but it is up to us to make it. He will instruct us on what we need to do, and we have to trust him through it. Psalm 32:8 (NIV) says, *I will instruct you and teach you in the way you should go; I will counsel you with my loving eye on you.* It will not be easy, and you will have to fight for it, because, as

I was asked, I am telling you, "You do not know what is tied to your obedience." There is something great on the other side of your God-led decisions if you are willing to trust him. The decisions you need to make will not always be easy or comfortable.

I have seen so much since I decided to go to China. Other people have been blessed through my move, and God has accelerated things in my own life because of it. God redeemed me through this experience. Although I did not get on the plane on my original date, God gave me another opportunity to say yes to his will, and I am so glad I did. This experience is unlocking doors that are tied to my future experiences. I have had friends tell me how my crazy faith and obedience to make this move has been inspiring and encouraging to them.

I had always dreamed of stepping away from corporate life to travel the world. This dream became a reality when I moved to China. During my time there, I visited seven countries. What literally would have taken me years to complete, God made happen within months. God has blessed me tremendously, not only in tangible things but in intangible ways. My faith in him has gone to new heights because of this experience. He has opened my mind in greater ways, and my trust in him has deepened. I have connected with people I would have never come across had I not taken this crazy leap of faith. My life is forever changed, and I think it is incredible that China is a puzzle piece in my story.

- ❖ **Reflect on your life:** Name something God is asking you to do? Are you willing to push through your fears to be obedient? Are you hesitating to obey? Why or why not? What if great and amazing things are on the other side of your crazy faith?

CHAPTER 15

Life Abroad

On May 2019, I arrived in Shanghai, China to teach English as a second language expecting to be there for a minimum of a year, but possibly longer. At thirty-six years old, I left my job as an accountant to relocate to China (yes, I have crazy faith and was willing to risk it all to move where God was leading me). Prior to physically going to China, I had prayed for years that I would take at least one year to travel the world. Side note: The power of your words is very real. Proverbs 18:21 (NKJV) says, *Death and life are in the power of the tongue, and those who love it will eat its fruit.*

I had a vision for my life, and it came to fruition when I went to China. Let me be clear—this move was the toughest move I have ever made in my life. It was very difficult to leave everything I had ever known to go to a place unknown, sight unseen, where I had never walked. People thought I was absolutely crazy, and well, I thought I was bat crazy too, but through it all, I knew God had a purpose for me.

I had only been working with this employer for two months, and I was terrified that I would never get hired there again, but that is how God works. I was willing to risk my reputation and my career to do what he was leading me to do. I was scared and nervous, but I knew he would guide me and that all would be well. I leaned heavily on Genesis 12:1 (NKJV): *Now the Lord had said to Abram: "Get out of your country, from your family and from your father's house, to a land that I will show you. I will make you a great nation; I will bless you and make your name great; and you shall be a blessing. I will bless those who bless you, and I will curse him who curses you; and in you all the families of the earth shall be blessed."* Where God guides, he provides.

Through all the tears of packing up my apartment and giving away everything I had owned, to reducing my life down from thirty-six years of accumulating tons of material things to three boxes and two suitcases, I knew my perspective on life would be forever changed. The physical release of all those material things created spiritual room in my life and in my mind. For the first time in my life that I can remember, I was truly surrendering to God's plan and letting go of what I thought life was supposed to look like. I stepped onto the United Airlines flight for an almost seventeen-hour flight and over 4,500 miles to go to a new land where I did not speak the language or know a single person. I knew I would be ok but wondered if I was absolutely crazy.

I remember sitting in my seat on the airplane thinking, "This is crazy, this is crazy, this is crazy." This is not a move typically made by a thirty-six-year-old; this is more common for the early twenty-something-year-old still exploring life and adventure. But this move was designed specifically for me. Sure, I had never taught before (in a school setting), but I would figure it out just as I had done with new things all my life. As I arrived in China, my heart was calm and at peace, and I pushed my way through to get through customs, collect my luggage, and head to the hotel to prepare for my new life. My employer placed us in a hotel for two weeks, and we had to find an apartment during this time. We spent hours upon hours apartment hunting in Shanghai, and although we did not know the city, we had to make a decision on the best place to live and go with it. Thankfully, apartments for foreigners typically come furnished, and we were intentional about choosing an apartment close to the metro train station and a bus stop.

Our apartment was a shared four-bedroom, two-bath apartment, meaning you would rent a room, the other rooms could have random strangers living in it, and we were sharing the bathrooms. This was an interesting situation. We had people constantly moving in and out. I believe they rented out one of the rooms like an Airbnb. We constantly had a new person in this room every two weeks. Some spoke English, some did not. Each morning when we woke up, a random person might come into the apartment, whether it was the landlord, a new person moving in, maintenance, or the cleaning lady. Coming from America, I wasn't accustomed to this experience, and they rarely informed us if someone would be in the apartment.

Also, the police occasionally checked to ensure those living there were registered to be there. We had to show them our passports and work visas. If an unregistered individual was in the apartment, they could face a fine. Learning the customs and rules of the Chinese culture was interesting. Their holidays are very different from the rest of the world, as they do not traditionally celebrate Thanksgiving or Christmas but rather Golden Week, Chinese New Year, Dragon Boat Festival, and Mid-Autumn Festival, just to name a few.

I went to Shanghai to teach English as a second language at a training center that was not affiliated with the school system but was considered an extracurricular activity. We typically taught in the evenings (after school hours), starting around 4 p.m., and on the weekends from 8 a.m. until 6 p.m. Teaching kids of a completely different culture was challenging but fun at times. The children, parents, and grandparents were often mesmerized that someone of my skin color was in China teaching. I will never forget on my very first day at the school, I was observing another teacher. As I walked into her classroom, this little girl walked up to me, grabbed my hand, and began to rub the backside of my hand. It was as if she were rubbing to see if the color of my skin would come off. She smiled but then looked confused and fascinated, then she smiled again. I continued to smile back at her, as my brown skin was not changing.

This was the beginning of receiving many looks and stares. I often rode the metro train or the bus, and locals took pictures of me or simply just stared at me in confusion. I found this to be quite annoying and exhausting most of the time, as the locals did not comprehend the concept of personal space. There was no verbal communication between us, and I often had to do my best to ignore the stares. A few times, locals touched my hair without warning or notice. One time, I was at the kiosk ordering my food at McDonald's, and I felt a tug on my hair. I turned around to an older woman holding a few of my braids in her hands, staring at them with a confused look on her face. She said something in Mandarin (which I did not understand), and then she walked off.

Another time, I was heading to work on the bus, and an older gentleman sat next to me. He brushed my hair with his fingers, and as I looked at him, he just smiled. I understand the people were curious and were not intentionally trying to be rude or offensive; however, at times, this was overwhelming. I preferred not to be touched by random strangers, especially without notice or warning. I did my best to smile through these moments, and a few times, I snapped pictures of them taking pictures of me. Through it all, I did run into some friendly locals who assisted me when I needed help. Kindness and a simple smile are universal, and even through the language barriers and cultural differences, this is always loved and appreciated no matter what country you are in. At the popular tourist attractions, I was often approached by a local interested in having a conversation—mostly wanting to discuss basketball and the forty-fifth president of the United States. These conversations were appreciated and welcomed.

I get so many questions about that experience, and I will answer some of the common questions below.

- Did I like living in China? Overall, I did not like living in China. Experiencing a different culture was great; however, I wouldn't want to stay there long term. China is obviously quite different than most other countries. There are a lot more restrictions on the people, and sometimes it was difficult for me to connect with family and friends back home due to government-applied restrictions on virtual private networks (VPNs).

- What was the most challenging thing about living there? The most challenging thing was dealing with racism and cultural differences. Never in my life had I experienced blatant racism in the workplace. They often made different exceptions for locals and those of fair skin color as opposed to those of us with darker skin color. Job ads posted on WeChat for teaching indicated "white teachers only," thus excluding everyone else. When it came to community-facing events, those of darker skin color were not chosen to participate. Even marketing material and ads posted throughout the city only showed those of fair skin color. We even had noticeable cultural differences between teachers and local and foreign staff. Foreign staff were generally firmer and applied the rules, while local teachers aimed to please everyone.

Many times, if a student misbehaved in the classroom, I would not give them a sticker for the day; however, when the parents went to the local teacher, they provided them with whatever was asked. This created division among the teachers because we should have been on the same wavelength when it came to the rules, and I was often called mean because I expected the students to follow the rules as we had established at the beginning of class, and I would not reward them for bad behavior as instructed.

- Did I travel while there? Traveling was one of the best parts of being in China. It brought me so much joy to explore this part of the world. I took trips to Singapore; Sanya, China; Phuket, Thailand; Ho Chi Minh City, Vietnam; Manila, Philippines; Cebu, Philippines; and Bali, Indonesia. The farthest destination was a six-hour flight, and traveling was fairly inexpensive. For most trips, I could purchase round-trip airfare for approximately $250.00 USD. Singapore was my favorite destination overall, but I would absolutely love to go back to the beaches in Thailand.

- How did I end up in China? I was on Instagram and had always followed the company's tour page. Intrigued and interested, I began to browse their website, which asked, "Are you ready to explore the world? It is waiting for you." I immediately connected with this (remember, I had been praying to travel the world for one year). The thought of still earning an income, health insurance, a work visa, have access to free Mandarin lessons, and twenty-one days of paid holidays made it a no-brainer for me. The job requirements were a bachelor's degree, a clear background check, the ability to live abroad for one year, a TEFL certification (which I earned through them once hired), and a passport that did not expire within the next six months. I easily met all these requirements.

  I applied in August 2019, and by September 2019, I was hired and began to prepare for my move abroad. This appeared to be an opportunity of a lifetime, and I could not pass this up. Upon arriving in China, I began to understand this opportunity was completely opposite of what they had indicated. The pay was well below the industry average for teaching positions, and I often had to reach into my own savings account to live comfortably. On a few occasions, my monthly paycheck was incorrect and contained errors that equated to missing funds. The company didn't immediately correct the errors, and I had to wait until the next month's pay cycle to see the correction. This happened on multiple occasions for me and was very frustrating.

- Would I live abroad again? I absolutely would. Although I did not love everything about my experience in China, God used this opportunity to open my mind to a new world of possibilities. It has given me the confidence that I can do anything in my life. And I firmly believe I was supposed to meet and connect with certain people along my path.

This means more... Going to China was bigger than relocating to an unknown physical place and traveling the world. It was the puzzle piece God used to expand my heart and mind. He exposed me to new cultures, new ways of doing things, and a new life. I broke free from my comfort zone and developed the boldness and courage to step out in faith. This experience caused a major shift in my perspective on life, and I am forever changed because of it. It showed me he has a big plan for my life, one I cannot even begin to comprehend, but I know and trust that as the journey continues, he will always lead me in the right direction. He has a plan for me greater than what my eyes can see. No matter what country I am living in, I know my provider and protector is walking with me. I am so glad I pressed through all the feelings of fear, doubt, and anxiety of stepping into this unknown territory. While I fully expected my experience in China to last for a full year, I returned to the States after nine months. Continue reading for why I returned earlier than planned.

- ❖ **Reflect on your life:** Are you open to exploring new and different experiences? Why or why not? Have you ever taken a leap of faith? Have you ever lived abroad, or do you desire to live abroad?

CHAPTER 16

The Year 2020

The year 2020 was an interesting year for this world and for our personal lives. I do not think I have met anyone who says they could have planned the year that way. It has reminded us that we are not in control, and no matter what we do, we cannot predict what will happen. So as life happens, we must roll with it and keep pressing on. For me, it was an incredible time to grow and I was filled with moments where I felt like my life did not make sense. I had moments of both sadness and excitement.

Earlier in the year, I asked God what he wanted me to do with my life at that point and time. My favorite scripture to turn to when I need guidance is Psalm 32:8 (NIV), which says, *I will instruct you and teach you in the way you should go; I will counsel you with my loving eye on you.* I prayed that scripture and heard a simple word: "serve." As you can imagine, serving can go in many different directions, so I began exactly where I was. When I heard that word from God, I was living in Grand Prairie, Texas with my cousin and his incredible family. This was a very unusual situation for me to be in.

Let us talk about how I got there: It was January 2020, and I was living and working in Shanghai, China. My friends and I had already planned to travel to the Philippines for the Chinese New Year in late January. A few weeks before we headed to the Philippines, news of the coronavirus starts to hit the media. At this point, it had not become anything to be concerned about, so I boarded my flight to the Philippines for a five-day trip. While in the Philippines enjoying an amazing and fun vacation, we received word from work that the school was closed until further notice and we could not return to work. We looked at this time as an amazing opportunity to visit another country of our dreams, so we booked a flight from Manila, Philippines to Bali, Indonesia. I am so glad I did because my original flight from the Philippines back to China ended up being canceled (this was the first of many flights to be canceled). I flew solo to Bali, Indonesia (day seven of my original planned five-day trip) as my other friends were coming the next day.

I originally left China on January 24, 2020 with five days' worth of clothes, fully expecting to return on January 30, 2020. When I arrived in Bali on January 31, 2020, it was day seven of my adventures, and we were scheduled to stay in Bali until February 8, 2020. My friends and I enjoyed an eight-day vacation in Bali, living our best lives and enjoying all the beaches and delicious food Bali had to offer (it was as amazing as it sounds). But in the back of my mind, I was starting to wonder how in the world all this would turn out. *Will I ever make it back to China? What is going to happen? Is this really my life right now? Wait, all my life is still in China; how will I get my belongings? Should I just go back to the United States?* I had question after question, so much to consider.

Here is my timeline of flights as I booked them:

January 24, 2020 – Shanghai, China > Manila, Philippines *(Flight time: 3h 45m)*
January 30, 2020 – Manila, Philippines > Shanghai, China (canceled)
This was my original flight for Chinese New Year, fully expecting a return to China.

January 27, 2019 – Manila, Philippines > Cebu, Philippines *(Flight time: 1h 30m)*
January 29, 2020 – Cebu, Philippines > Manila, Philippines *(Flight time: 1h 25m)*
Part of the original plans for our vacation.

March 11, 2020 – Shanghai, China > Seattle, Washington (canceled)
March 11, 2020 – Seattle, Washington > Houston, Texas (canceled)
Earlier in 2020, I had already decided to relocate back to the States. This was my original flight for my return.

February 3, 2020 - Shanghai, China > Hong Kong (canceled)
February 3, 2020 - Hong Kong > Bali, Indonesia (canceled)
February 9, 2020 - Bali, Indonesia > Hong Kong (canceled)
February 9, 2020 - Hong Kong > Shanghai, China (canceled)

After we were delayed at work, we thought, Well, let us go back to China, get more clothes, and prepare for another fun adventure in Bali; however, this flight was canceled as well.

January 31, 2020 - Manila, Philippines > Bali, Indonesia *(Flight time: 4h 14m)*
February 8, 2020 - Bali Indonesia > Manila, Philippines *(Flight time: 3h 50m)*

At this point, going back to China seemed almost impossible, so we just made the best of it and went directly from Manila to Bali instead.

February 8, 2020 - Manila, Philippines > Taipei, Taiwan *(Flight time: 2h 20m)*

I thought I would be smart and possibly go through Taiwan to return to Shanghai. However, I ended up leaving Taiwan to head back to the States instead.

February 9, 2020 - Taipei, Taiwan > Hong Kong (canceled)
February 10, 2020 - Hong Kong > Shanghai, China (canceled)
February 11, 2020 - Hong Kong > Taipei, Taiwan (canceled)
February 11, 2020 - Shanghai, China > Hong Kong (canceled)

I was not outrunning COVID-19, yet another flight cancellation.

February 8, 2020 - Taipei, Taiwan > San Francisco, California *(Flight time: 11h)*
February 8, 2020 - San Francisco, California > Houston, Texas *(Flight time: 3h 54m)*

After all the circling and flight cancellations, I was feeling that nudge in my spirit that the safest thing for me was to return to the States. I almost did not make this flight due to the previous flight running late, but by the grace of God, I made it. And it was the smoothest flight of all.

February 11, 2020 - Houston, Texas > Midland, Texas

I had to take yet another flight. This time, I had to fly to my dad's house to pick up my car. This was the last flight I was on before COVID-19 shut down the States.

As the timeline presents, this was an intense, fun, scary, and crazy time in my life. Since I had returned to the States, my lease on my apartment in China was up in May 2020, and I coordinated with friends to clean out my apartment and pack up the most important belongings. (Sidenote: I have the most amazing friends, who cleaned out my apartment for me). I decided to release those material things that could be replaced much easier than trying to mail them (i.e., clothes, shoes, etc.). Whoever has the clothes and shoes I could not keep, I hope they are enjoying them.

As of October 21, 2020, a few of the items I could keep were still in China (my laptop, important personal documents, GoPro, etc.). As you can imagine, trying to ship anything had not been the easiest task, especially when dealing with electronics. At this moment, I have emotionally detached from those things, and while I would like to get my belongings one day, I have absolutely no idea if or when that would ever happen.

Since I have returned from China, God has taken me through times of pruning and restoration. As I spent time with my family in Dallas, God worked on my heart and exposed my ugly places. I had definitely walked with a lot of pride tucked deep into my heart. I was raised to not depend on anyone but myself and to make things happen for myself, so to be in a situation now where I had no choice but to depend on someone else was a tough adjustment for me. I really thought I would only be in Dallas for maybe two weeks or so, BUT GOD had other plans when I ended up being there for six months. Initially, I tried to fight God on this because I was once again completely out of my comfort zone and wanted my own space; however, God had other plans.

Through this time, I spent tons of time with my cousin and his family, and I also got closer to my biological sisters (which had been my prayer request years prior). Being able to call my big sisters was very new for me. My family dynamic has been tough over the last two decades, BUT GOD is bringing restoration to my family, and I am forever grateful to be here to live it, see it, and participate in it. God is truly incredible. My cousin and I spent moments talking about life and some of our greatest losses. My brother died in 2000 from an accident, and his sister (my cousin) passed away in 2016. Their lives were a testimony and encouragement for so many others. So my cousin and I talked about our feelings surrounding those losses and bonded in a whole new way than ever before.

I learned firsthand what it takes to have a family, to get an idea of how I wanted to manage my household and the energy I want to set for my house. Let me just say this, parents have a *tough* job, and I could not even begin to imagine what it is like for those with only one parent in the household. I experienced firsthand the chaos of raising three beautiful and very active children (two being under the age of five). Whew, let me just be honest, I drank wine every night. And let's not even discuss the potty-training stage for a two-year-old.

Let me place this pin right here—*God Bless All The Parents*. ☺ As if managing the household daily is not enough, then you have to add going to work and maintaining a marriage through it all. Just wow! To all my parents, I now understand why sometimes you just let your child scream in the grocery store or run around inside of Ross and Marshall's. You must be intentional about the battles you choose with your children, and sometimes it is just not worth the fight.

This means more… What an unprecedented year 2020 was. As I reflect on that year, I was reminded that God is in control of it all, and no human being can do anything to stop the plans he has already laid out. I am grateful for the opportunity to slow down and reflect on what is most important, which does not involve money but, rather, relationships—relationships with my Heavenly Father, family, and friends. For years, I have prayed to develop a solid relationship with my biological sisters. If I am honest, I was not sure this was even possible because of the chaos we had lived in for so long. I even stopped praying for this years ago, and in 2020, everything started to change and restoration is happening. We are communicating more than ever before and being intentional about connecting.

This was not the year to gather more stuff but, rather, appreciate what I have. God had a plan all along. Even though I could not see it, he already knew the way in which he would bring us back together. Jeremiah 29:11-12 (NKJV): *For I know the thoughts that I think toward you, says the L*ORD*, thoughts of peace and not of evil, to give you a future and a hope. Then you will call upon Me and go and pray to Me, and I will listen to you.*

- ❖ **Reflect on your life:** As you reflect on your Year 2020, what are your thoughts? Do you believe God has a specific plan and purpose for your life? Why or why not?

CHAPTER 17

The Restoration Process

What an incredible and historic day November 7, 2020 was. I was out shopping as news broke of our forty-sixth President and that Vice President Kamala Harris, the first African American woman, had made history. This brought me so much joy and empowerment as a woman. What seemed impossible for centuries literally became possible right in front of our own eyes. This day was also special because my new living room was installed in my apartment. You may be asking why my new living room is so special, and my only response is *restoration* happened right before my eyes. What seemed impossible for the longest was now manifesting itself and became a physical reality for me.

Remember, before I moved to China in 2019, I gave away almost *everything* I owned. I left for China with thirty-six years of my life packed into three boxes that I sent to my dad's house and two suitcases that went to China with me. It was a moment of release and surrender of things in my life that were not important to where God was calling me. I was certain that I would be abroad for years to come and had no idea I would return to the States just nine months later. Due to the start of the pandemic, I came back to the States, and in the midst of traveling, the few items I did have were also left behind in China.

As I reflect on that time, I see God literally breaking down all the old things of my life for me to completely surrender in order to rebuild me how he wants. I did not recognize this as a rebuilding opportunity amid the situation. I laughed about leaving my belongings, and it certainly was crazy times. At the same time, I was overwhelmed with a great sense of peace. I continued to speak and believe that God would restore me and supply all my needs according to his riches and glory by Christ Jesus (Philippians 4:19 NKJV). I had no idea when or where he would, but I just believed he would do it for me.

Let me tell you, this rebuilding is ten times better than anything I could have ever thought of or imagined. As I mentioned earlier, upon my return to the States, I lived with family for six months because I had nothing. I could not even find employment for a solid six months, but God allowed me to continue to live in abundance and out of an overflow. As things began to shift and before I received the job offer, I felt led to move back to Houston. It was a step of faith as well. I knew God was calling me back to this city.

I received my official job offer on August 6, 2020, the very same day I decided to relocate (I had a great birthday indeed! ☺). Although I signed my job offer letter, I still needed to go through the pre-employment screening and background check, which we were told could take up to six to eight weeks to complete (especially due to the impact the pandemic was having on businesses); therefore, I did not have an official start date yet.

I searched for apartments, expecting to move in on or around September 1. I developed a list of important priorities during my apartment search—location, within my budget, and a place where I would feel safe. I enlisted the assistance of an apartment locater to help narrow down my options of apartments because Houston is a very big city with numerous living options. After viewing a few communities, I knew when I walked onto this property, this would be my home. I inquired about a September 1 move-in and viewed a few of their amazing available options. Something in me was still a bit unsettled about the first unit, so I asked my best friend to come with me to view the community a week later. I also continued viewing other properties but had no interest because I already knew where I should be.

On August 14, 2020, as we were discussing everything about this unit, she was unsettled also, so we viewed another unit with a pool view.

The Restoration Process

Seeing the pool view changed everything; however, I did not like the white cabinets in this unit, so we searched the online portal for other available units. One more unit drew my interest, but it was available now and I had to secure it now. I could not wait until September 1 because the pricing increased; therefore, if I wanted this unit, I would have to move in on August 17, 2020. I thought I might encounter some trouble with leasing since I had no rental history for the last year and a half, but the process flowed smoothly.

On August 17, 2020, I was moving into my new apartment. I believed God for September 1, and he showed me that he could accelerate whatever timing I had planned. How did I allow myself to be so uneasy and impatient, only for him to accelerate the timing to begin with? What if we choose simply to rest, knowing that God has all the details already worked out? I understand our humanness, but how many times have we encountered situations where we worried for nothing because of our impatience and frankly lack of trust in God (even though he has proven himself repeatedly). What if we simply begin to take him at his word!

For almost three months after moving in, I sat in an empty apartment. At one point, I had an air mattress that I borrowed from my best friend, but eventually, the air ducts busted. I ordered a brand-new bed from Ashley Furniture but had issues with the delivery, so I ended up sleeping on the hard floor for a while. I was upset and annoyed with my delivery issues but humbled by sleeping on the floor. So to say I appreciate this apartment and space on a whole new level is an understatement. I am humbled, grateful, and honored to walk through this restoration process. I am so glad I did not rush this process because of impatience. I cried and pressed through moments of wondering if God had forgotten about me, all to realize he was there the entire time. He is an on-time God, and he has not failed me yet. I knew I wanted my space to be nice and very special, so I began to think about using an interior designer.

During this time, I was completing the onboarding process for my employment and still had no official start date. I continued to press on for a few weeks and fielded a few questions on my background. Most questions centered around my employment in China and obtaining an employment verification. For a moment, I was slightly nervous this may be an issue, but with assistance from friends, I got what I needed. I began work with my new employer on August 31, 2020 as a Senior Financial Analyst. Thankfully, we were working from home, which is an enjoyable experience for me.

This means more… This process had nothing to do with material things or even employment. Through this process, I saw God's hand over my life and his continued work to restore to me ten times everything I lost, gave up, and let go of. I feel blessed, humbled, and grateful for the process. Sure, some moments have been hard and I felt forgotten, BUT GOD was there the entire time. This gave me the opportunity to truly depend on him in a way I had never done before. I am thankful for this journey. And as I write, the restoration process is only just beginning. I am a passenger on God's boat. He is the captain and knows the direction in which we are headed. I will trust him in the process and watch him give me *beauty for my ashes and the oil of joy for mourning, the garment of praise for the spirit of heaviness; that they may be called trees of righteousness, the planting of the Lord, that he may be glorified"* Isaiah 61:3 (NKJV).

- ❖ **Reflect on your life:** Have you felt like God was breaking you down? What was the situation? As you reflect, how can you see God's hand in the situation? How has He been rebuilding you?

CHAPTER 18

A Life of Faith

God has a plan for your life! As you look back over your life, what puzzle pieces or nuggets has he left for you along the way? How do you define your story? Where have you seen his grace and mercy in your situations? Psalm 16:11 says, *You will show me the path of life; in your presence is fullness of joy and at your right hand are pleasures forevermore.* Our entire lives are being orchestrated by God for his plan and purpose. He is using the good, the bad, and the ugly to help shape and mold us. Romans 8:28 *reminds us that all things work together for the good of those who love the Lord, to those who are called according to His purpose.* It is all coming together even when it does not feel like it makes sense or is painful.

> *For you created my inmost being; you knit me together in my mother's womb. I praise you because I am fearfully and wonderfully made; your works are wonderful, I know that full well. My frame was not hidden from you when I was made in the secret place, when I was woven together in the depths of the earth. Your eyes saw my unformed body; all the days ordained for me were written in your book before one of them came to be (Psalm 139:13-16 NIV).*

Our lives are filled with various puzzle pieces, and slowly but surely, they are coming together to form a beautiful picture that we celebrate as your life. Your life experiences are not coincidences; they are being used to propel you into your destiny and purpose. The structure and meaning of your life were established from the very beginning by God. In the book, *Draw the Circle*, author Mark Batterson writes, "Redeem past experiences and recycle them for future opportunities." From the places where I excelled and lacked, God has allowed me to pursue my purpose and help others. I strongly encourage you to take inventory of your own life and see that it has purpose and God is with you the entire way.

This truly all means more, its bigger than anything we could ever think or imagine.

Let's Connect

Tag me on social media and let me know about the puzzle pieces in your life. I would love to hear your revelations, takeaways, and questions.

Purchase a copy or two for your friends and colleagues.

Website: www.ninaevansllc.com

Instagram: @ninevansllc

Facebook: @ninevansllc

Email: info@ninevansllc.com

Financial Coaching

Are you ready to make a change in your finances? Are you ready for financial freedom? Are you tired of making payments to creditors each month? Are you using a budget?

If your answer is yes to one or more of these questions...I am your financial champion and I am ready to assist you on your journey to financial freedom.

Visit my website for services: www.ninaevansllc.com

About the Author

Nina Evans is an author and money expert specializing in making the complex and sometimes boring financial concepts come alive in fun and tangible ways. Nina works with corporations and nonprofits to streamline their financial processes, understand their cash flow, and create a sustainable money workflow. Nina is passionate about guiding people out of debt and into financial freedom.

A few years ago, she found herself buried in $105,000 worth of credit card debt, student loans, and auto loans. One day she realized that she'd had enough of seeing her hard-earned money go to everyone else's pockets but hers. At that moment she decided to take matters into her own hands.

With a background in accounting in the oil and gas industry, she knew exactly what to do. She laid out a plan for her financial goals and began her journey to rid herself of a mountain of debt. That plan has now evolved into the Financial Champion System where she makes the complex and sometimes confusing, easy with a clear plan to move from overwhelm to financial freedom.

Nina supports small businesses and non-profits with consulting services. She takes those with outdated, inefficient, or non-existent financial systems and sets them up to have a clear, well-rounded view of their money - ultimately making tax season a breeze.

Nina is the author of the book, *This Means More*, where she encourages readers to take inventory of their life to recognize the many different pieces that shaped who they have become. She believes that everything has a purpose and plan and that every circumstance and trial is significant on the path to more.

Nina started her collegiate career at Cisco Junior College where she served as volleyball captain for two years. She moved on to graduate with honors from Texas Southern University with a Bachelor of Business Administration, Accounting. While at TSU, she served as volleyball team captain, was a part of Academic All-SWAC First Team, 2nd Team All-SWAC and the Student-Athlete Advisory Council (SAAC). Nina led as President of Beta Alpha Psi Honor Society, National Association of Black Accountants, and Golden Key International Honour Society. She continued her educational pursuits to earn a Master's of Business Administration with an emphasis in Accounting from Texas Women's University. Since graduating, she has been honored as an Inspired Energy Top Ten Finalist out of 1,500+ employees at a major organization.

Nina continues to create new experiences through travel. She's traveled to eleven countries and counting.

www.ingramcontent.com/pod-product-compliance
Lightning Source LLC
Chambersburg PA
CBHW071501070526
44578CB00001B/405